36

Oh, where did you get the delicious Honey Cakes?

Your visitors and the children will really enjoy these. They're so satisfying, so healthful, so economical —that you should keep a supply always handy.

And for your Bread, Party cakes and Smallgoods, you can always rely on our products. Drop in today.

K. L. & J. D. STOODL[EY]
Bakers and Confectioners,

H. H. Mertin, Angaston

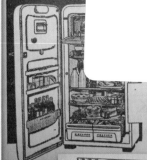

Washing Machines
Records.
E.R. Batteries
☆
Trade-ins; Easy Terms
☆
Electrically yours for Sales and Service.
From
H. H. MERTIN

100 FERGUSON TRACTORS ARE WORKING IN THIS AREA

FARM FASTER, CHEAPER AND BETTER WITH

FERGUSON

CHARLESTON GARAGE & FARM SERVICES
Phone Lobethal 89

ROYLO
THE ROYAL RESERVE
PORT OF *Orlando*

try it —
— as a nightcap...
Home from the theatre... a quick supper snack, then, just before bed, a soothing, satisfying glass of Roylo.

with cake for 'elevenses'...
Mid-morning or afternoon is the time for a slice of cake and a glass of light and mellow Roylo.

with dessert, or after dinner...
For that "little bit better" to make your meal memorable, serve Roylo, the perfect port for every occasion.

as a warming glass in the cold weather...
One warming sip is sufficient to see you'll move on without pulling... Roylo — the Royal Reserve Port of Orlando.

you'll know **ROYLO**

It was a **marvellous salad...** made with **real** vinegar

Seppelts
WINE VINEGAR

Save time & trouble — serve...

Berri PURE FRUIT JUICES

VITAMIN CONTENT GUARANTEED

Busy mothers save hours by serving BERRI Pure Fruit Juices. Poured straight from hygienic taste-free cans, these delicious unadulterated fruit juices contain every healthful vitamin growing bodies need. There is no squeezing, no peeling, no waste, no work.

ORANGE — GRAPEFRUIT
APRICOT — TOMATO
Obtainable Everywhere

A perfect treat...

delicious, creamy
AMSCOL ICE CREAM
In cones, on sticks, wafers or dandies.
It's a food—not a fad

FARMERS' CENTRE PTY LTD
— Keith —
PHONE: 17 (a.h. 247 or 160)
HOLDEN DEALERS

TRADE UP NOW TO THE NEW HT HOLDEN

72

Section D: POULTRY

Convener: B. Hart, Stewards: A. Sanderson, M. Nicolai, J. Cadzow, B. Batchelor.

Entries close Saturday, September 21. All birds hatched since July 1, 1967, will be eligible for cockerel and pullet classes only. Two trophies, valued at $1 each, donated by Mr. W. Lintvelt, for best male and female in show.
Watervalley Trophy for best Sussex female, value $2.
K. M. McInnis Trophy for best Sussex mal, value $2.
C. B. Hack Trophy for most points in Bantam Section, value

73

SHOW PRIZE LIST.

Judges Prefer..

WEST END EXPORT STOUT

It's the Extra CAR[E] THAT WI[LL] THE EXT[RA] BIDS!

Consign Your
STOCK
and
WOOL
to

FARMERS' UNION
THE S.A. FARMERS' CO-OPERATIVE UNION, LTD.
36 FRANKLIN STREET, ADELAIDE, S.A.
AT YOUR SERVICE
30 BRANCHES — OVER 400 AGENTS

Help the Show to be a S[uccess]

BOTTLE SOME FRUIT

IN YOUR OWN HOME

SECURE A

FOWLER'S

"VACOLA" Fruit and Vegetable Bottling Outfit, and realise how simple and easy it is to obtain perfect results with the patent—

Vacuum Self-Filling Bottles

[—Obtainable from all Stores throughout Australia.

WAKEFIELD PRESS

Liz Harfull grew up in the small farming community of Mil Lel, near Mount Gambier, where her family settled in the 1860s. She trained as a journalist at the local newspaper, later working at the Adelaide *Advertiser* and the *Stock Journal*. She has also worked as a public relations consultant.

Liz lives in the Adelaide Hills where she is busy as an author, freelance journalist, photographer and consultant. A keen amateur cook who thinks whipping up afternoon tea for friends is a great way to relax at the weekend, Liz has maintained her love of country shows since she was a child and lived just a few small paddocks away from the local showground.

For Mark and Karen
Some Aussie classics to test your skills
Happy cooking!
Liz Harfull

THE Blue Ribbon COOKBOOK

Liz Harfull

Recipes, stories and tips from prizewinning country show cooks

Wakefield Press
16 Rose Street
Mile End
South Australia 5031
www.wakefieldpress.com.au

First published 2008
Reprinted 2008, 2009, 2010, 2014

Copyright © Liz Harfull, 2008

All rights reserved. This book is copyright. Apart from any fair dealing for the purposes of private study, research, criticism or review, as permitted under the Copyright Act, no part may be reproduced without written permission. Enquiries should be addressed to the publisher.

Edited by Kathy Sharrad, Wakefield Press
Designed by Liz Nicholson, designBITE
Typeset by Clinton Ellicott, Wakefield Press
Printing and quality control in China by Tingleman Pty Ltd

ISBN 978 1 86254 792 6

This publication has been supported by the Royal Agricultural and Horticultural Society of South Australia and the Agricultural Societies Council of South Australia.

Previous page: James Bowd with his family's home produce display at the 1913 Mount Gambier Show (MD)

Agricultural Societies Council of SA Inc.

To my mother, Elaine, a great cook in her own right, and in memory of my father, Lyall, who always appreciated good baking.

Preface 1

Author's Note 11

Contents

STATE COMPETITION – Rich Fruit Cake 12

ADELAIDE – 16

ADELAIDE – Chocolate Orange Swirls 20

ADELAIDE – Cockles 22

ADELAIDE – Tomato Sauce 24

ANGASTON – Mumma's Rote Grütze 26

BALAKLAVA – Mango Diabetic Fruit Cake 30

BORDERTOWN – Eggplant and Chilli Chutney 32

BURRA – Lemon Slice 34

CALLINGTON – Curried Zucchini Relish 36

CLARE – Chocolate Crackles 38

CLEVE – Zucchini, Apple and Carrot Muffins 42

COONALPYN – Homemade Bread 44

CRYSTAL BROOK – Coffee Kisses 46

CUMMINS – Quince Jelly 48

EUDUNDA – Honey Biscuits 50

GAWLER – Rock Buns 54

JAMESTOWN – Banana Cake 58

Contents continued

KADINA – Cornflake Biscuits 62

KAPUNDA – Mustard Pickle 66

KEITH – Lemonade Scones 68

KIMBA – Chocolate Cupcakes 70

KINGSCOTE – Economical Steamed Plum Pudding 72

KINGSTON – Raspberry Jam Roll 74

LOXTON – Cinnamon Coffee Cake 78

LUCINDALE – Fig Jam 82

MAITLAND – Maud's Ginger Apricot Crunch 84

MANNUM – Pinch of Salt Sponge 86

MELROSE – Boiled Fruit Cake 88

MIL LEL – Chocolate Peppermint Slice 92

MILLICENT – Nestor's Yeast Buns 94

MINLATON – Cumquat Marmalade 98

MOUNT BARKER – Sue's Sausage Rolls 102

MOUNT GAMBIER – Ginger Fluff 106

MOUNT PLEASANT – Mary's Farm Pasties 110

MUNDULLA – Sultana Cake 114

MURRAY BRIDGE – Dried Apricot Jam 116

ORROROO – Macadamia and Wattle Seed Biscuits 118

PARNDANA – Genoa Cake 122

PENOLA – Anzac Biscuits 124

PINNAROO – Chocolate Layer Cake 128

PORT ELLIOT – Grandma's Chocolate Fudge Cake 132

PORT LINCOLN – Fruit and Nut Loaf 136

QUORN – Moderator's Slice 138

RENMARK – Orange Cake 140

STRATHALBYN – Carrot Cake 144

SWAN REACH – Jenny's Grape Jam 146

TANUNDA – German Yeast Cake 148

URAIDLA – Apple Squares 152

WHYALLA – Cream Puffs 156

WILMINGTON – Lemon Butter 158

WUDINNA – Honey Sponge Roll 160

YALLUNDA FLAT – Jubilee Cake 162

YANKALILLA – Chicken Cheesecake 166

How to be a Prizewinning Show Cook 170

Guide to Image Credits 171

Index 172

Top: Inspecting cereal sheaves at the Balaklava Show (PP) **Above:** Collecting show bags at the Royal Adelaide Show (HW)
Right, top: Shearing at the Balaklava Show (PP) **Right, bottom:** Showjumping at the 2008 Angaston Show

Preface

It is fifteen minutes to midnight and I am waiting for my third attempt at a respectable jubilee cake to come out of the oven. The kitchen is a mess. Mixing bowls, greaseproof paper and packets of ingredients vie for space on the wooden benchtop. Two earlier tries at baking the deceptively simple-looking recipe are cowering in one corner. A more successful batch of scones rests triumphant on the dresser, tops golden brown and bottoms dutifully free of flour.

I am cooking for my first agricultural show and so far it's been a mixed experience. It all seemed pretty straightforward when the book listing competitive classes arrived in the post for my local show. Flicking past sections for horses in action, floral art and pot plants, I came to cookery and preserves. What would it be? I decided to go with two traditional favourites in the world of show cooking – plain scones (a collection of four) and jubilee cake, an economical fruit cake that means I wouldn't be wasting too many expensive ingredients if I had to make several attempts to get it right. Just as well . . .

Agricultural shows are an important part of community life across Australia. In country areas they give people an excuse to get off the farm and catch up with the neighbours. In cities, events like the Royal Adelaide Show are both a spectacle and an institution that bring the city and the bush together for a few brief spring days.

But for many individuals they represent much more than an opportunity to relax and have fun. They are about the serious business of rewarding effort and enterprise – for both professional farmers setting out to produce the bestquality food crops and livestock, and talented amateurs keen to showcase their skills in a wide range of endeavours, from nurturing the perfect dahlia to breeding the perfect chook. Most of Australia's shows were founded by enthusiastic pioneers keen to see the new colony prosper by encouraging settlers to adopt the latest agricultural practices, nurture productive gardens and develop their homemaking skills.

The South Australian Agricultural Society's first recorded show was held in a hotel yard in Grenfell Street on 8 December 1840, just four years after the arrival of the first European settlers in South Australia.

Top: Riding the 'Cha Cha' (PP)

Above: Hamilton Boulevard crowd at the Royal Adelaide Show (HW)

It was a modest event, exhibiting a small range of produce, including wheat, oats, barley, maize, cheese, potatoes and onions. Over the next 40 years the concept quickly spread across the colony, from Mount Gambier, which held its first formal show in 1861, to Mount Barker (1847) and Quorn (1880). A spate of shows rippled into life along the River Murray in the early 1900s, followed by further surges after the two world wars as new farmland was opened up through soldier settler and land development schemes.

The concept expanded rapidly from mid-week ploughing competitions and demonstrations of agricultural machinery into full one- two- and even three-day programs celebrating diverse agricultural, horticultural and floricultural achievements. Competitive classes were created for everything from saddlery making to hand-stitching lace petticoat. Each farm family would spend hours selecting produce and arranging it in intricate displays of renaissance splendour. Patrons would crowd into halls and marquees to see the collections, tables groaning with home-cured meats, farmhouse butter and cheeses, sheaves of wheat, fresh and preserved fruit and vegetables, baskets of eggs, loaves of bread, and bottles of homemade beers, wines and sauces.

Surprisingly, available records indicate that it took many decades for cookery to emerge as a skill worthy of its own competitive section. The earliest schedules reveal that often the only baking classes were for staple items like bread, listed in general produce classes. Things started to change by the early 1900s. Newspaper reports of the Eudunda Show in 1907, for example, note Mrs W. T. Kamm produced the best German cake and Mrs J. von Bertouch the best collection of pastry.

Each show took a slightly different approach, often influenced by the cultural backgrounds of immigrants who first settled in the area. Dill cucumbers, pickled onions, yeast cakes and honey biscuits brought German traditions to Barossa Valley shows. Although they are disappearing, pasties were once popular at Burra and in Yorke Peninsula's Copper Triangle where Cornish miners plied their trade.

The nature of commercial food crops grown locally was another influencing factor at early shows, and is still reflected in today's schedules. In the Riverland, the Loxton Show boasts a wonderful array of citrus marmalades; and there is a special rose jam class at Renmark, the home of Australia's largest rose garden. Honey classes are popular on Kangaroo Island, and in the Adelaide Hills there are special prizes for recipes using apples and pears.

Top: Early postcard of the Clare Show (NTSA, Clare district)

Above: Mr H. Hirth with pots of orchids at the Mount Gambier Show, 1960 (SLSA: BRG 347/1950)

Top: *Agricultural and Horticultural Show, Adelaide,* watercolour by S. T. Gill, 1843 (AGSA)
Left: An exhibit at the 1910 Uraidla Show (USHFSI)
Above: Country show at Minlaton, 1910 (SLSA: B 41666)

Previous page: Doecke family home produce display, Angaston Show, 2007

Below: Chocolate crackle making

A study of cookery schedules over the decades also reveals how classes have changed over time to reflect trends in domestic cooking. The early 1900s featured delicacies virtually unheard of today, like seed, Red Indian, ribbon and pound cakes, and an incredible array of pickles and jams. Today, banana, chocolate and carrot cakes, muffins and mud cakes, cafe-trendy friands and almond bread keep the patrons drooling. Pizzas and quiche joined the savoury line-up some time ago, while only a few shows still offer you a chance to try your hand at Cornish pasties or meat pies.

Or you can test your skills making pestos, Asian-style sweet chilli sauces and fruit leathers in preserves sections, usually run separately from cookery. This is where you also get to see more traditional jars of preserved fruits and vegetables, with their contents carefully arranged in neat rows and symmetrical patterns. Our Mediterranean climate is reflected in more traditional classes – almost every South Australian show caters for apricot and fig jams, marmalades, tomato sauce and lemon butter (or lemon cheese as it is known in some areas).

In a worrying indication of the emergence of diabetes as a major health issue for Australians, shows also offer special classes for diabetic cakes. More concerning to many traditional cooks, who take it as confirmation that the art of baking is fast being lost, some shows even have classes for cakes made from packet mixes, mainly for children. It is an attempt to get them started on something relatively simple, especially in households where their parents would have to make a special trip to the supermarket to buy baking ingredients. Others take heart in the undying popularity of junior classes for chocolate and honey crackles, pikelets, chocolate cakes, scones and decorated cupcakes.

In an innovative approach to generate fresh enthusiasm and increase entries, shows have also introduced a range of novelty classes. The most popular are men's only cake competitions, with chocolate cake classes an outright favourite with the blokes, who are no doubt highly motivated to have a go at making something they love to eat. If you fit the criteria you can try your hand at president's competitions, open to anyone who is president of a local community organisation. And at Burra you get to decorate a cake in your footy team's colours. Apart from individual items, there have also been trends over the years towards collections and 'special occasion' trays created around themes such as father's luncheon; today's equivalent is the truckies lunch competition at Coonalpyn.

Some classes remain perennial favourites. Scones, sponge cakes and rolls, lamingtons and cream puffs are found on almost every show schedule. Bread is making a resurgence and there is renewed interest in preserves, particularly classes for tomato sauce and jam making. But there is no doubt the pinnacle of achievement in the world of show cooking is the fruit cake, in its myriad forms. If you really want to test your mettle and earn the right to stand alongside the finest cooks, you cannot avoid the rich fruit cake, the genoa cake or the sultana cake.

So who makes the effort to enter? The cooks in this collection range in age from three to 93. They come from a variety of backgrounds. Most have been inspired by their mothers and grandmothers; there are several family 'dynasties' with three generations competing against each other in friendly rivalry. And it's not all up to the women. Men seem to be taking an increasing interest and are often well represented in preserves sections. Junior classes for both primary and secondary students are incredibly popular, especially where local schools offer encouragement. Boys and girls compete alongside each other, and often in equal ratio, but only a handful will stick with it once they leave school and have to take on more experienced cooks in the open classes.

And the reward for all their efforts? Well, it's definitely not the money. Prizes for most classes have failed to keep up with inflation. At Cleve in the 1950s you could win as much as 20 shillings for a first prize, compared with just $6 today, while many other shows are offering only $1 or $2. Entry fees are often as low as 50 cents but unless you have your own chickens, the cost of baking most entries outstrips the monetary rewards.

So why do they do it? Don't let them fool you. Even the cook who reminds you of your grandmother or Aunty Margaret is often fiercely competitive. Put simply, most love to win, and they all get a genuine buzz from walking into the show hall after the judging has been completed to see if there is a prize card or championship ribbon perched against their entry. Many volunteer as stewards or convenors to help organise exhibition sections, and they all love their show and want to see the tradition maintained for future generations. Too many have already been lost because of declining rural populations, lack of volunteers, and increasing regulations and costs.

Like their colonial forebears, they also gain enormous satisfaction from achieving a level of perfection that only comes from attention to

Top: Watching the junior cookery judging at the Royal Adelaide Show (HW)

Above: Prizewinners in the sausage roll class at Port Elliot

Top: Slice judging at the Royal Adelaide Show (HW)

Above: The grand champion preserve at Strathalbyn

detail. And therein lies the difference between being a show cook and cooking at home. As more than one show cook explained, this is not about cooking for shearers where you need large proportions to feed an appetite fuelled by hard physical work, it's about presentation and dainty confections worthy of high tea at the Ritz. 'There are two definitions of cooking – afternoon tea or shearing shed, and show cooking is afternoon tea,' one competitor told me.

That, in turn, has led to the evolution of a set of judging criteria foreign to most of us: marks on the bottom of your cake from using a wire rack to cool it are an absolute no-no; paper linings for cake pans must be cut precisely (some cooks even iron the paper – wrinkle marks on the side of your rich fruit cake could be all that separates you from the state championship); and while traces of flour might add a rustic touch to home-cooked scones, they are not appreciated in a competition.

Anyone can enter any show; all you have to do is contact your local show society and get hold of a current show book. Most country shows have these available a few weeks before the event, and you can often enter right up to a week before the show. Larger shows, like the Royal Adelaide Show, close off entries many weeks in advance. In South Australia, you can find out more at www.sacountryshows.com, or, for the Royal Adelaide Show, www.adelaideshowground.com.au.

Judging sessions are usually closed to the public, but becoming involved as a volunteer steward or helper gives you a chance to learn by watching some of the most experienced and capable cooks in the country tip, cut, sniff, snap, crumble and taste their way through all the entries. Alternatively, get to know an experienced show cook and ask their advice. Most are very generous with their knowledge because they are keen to encourage others to become involved and discover the joys of cooking and competing. It was the main reason most of the cooks in this book agreed to let me into their kitchens and share their best-kept secrets. And it worked. After a sleepless night worrying about letting them down and disgracing the display cased at my local show, I won first prize for my scones and second prize for the jubilee cake. 'That's it, you're hooked,' a smiling cooking convenor warned me.

Top: Judging cakes at the Royal Adelaide Show (HW)

Above: Millicent Show ribbons

Right: A steward counts entries in an open cake class at the Royal Adelaide Show

Author's Note

This book would not have been possible without the generous support, goodwill and enthusiasm of its two major sponsors – the Royal Agricultural and Horticultural Society of South Australia and the Agricultural Societies Council of South Australia.

I would also like to thank the state's country show societies for their unflagging support and encouragement in helping identify local cooks, and source information and illustrations. Many hundreds of volunteers willingly donate their energy and time to organise outstanding events, despite increasing pressures and often diminishing resources, and to keep alive a precious tradition that has contributed so much to the rich tapestry of community life in South Australia.

Special thanks to Joan Graham who kindly gave permission to use her two books, *Cooking for Competition* and *The Show Bench: The Exhibitors' Guide* as references for judges tips.

Invaluable assistance has also been provided by the staff of the Royal Agricultural and Horticultural Society of South Australia, including archivist Marilyn Ward and the team at Rural Services, in particular Malcolm Buckby and Brad Ward. Special thanks also to Richard Fewster and John Rothwell for their assistance in getting the project started and ongoing encouragement.

A large team of volunteer test cooks contributed countless hours, bags of flour, eggs, butter and kilos of fruit to trying every recipe in this book, and providing invaluable feedback. My undying gratitude to you all, in particular my sister, Fiona Wooldridge.

My personal thanks to my family and friends for their ongoing patience, love and support; and to the highly professional team at Wakefield Press, who have helped to make my first publishing experience as an author a great joy.

And lastly and most of all, a heartfelt thanks to the wonderful cooks featured in this book for their extraordinary cooperation, passion and patience in sharing their stories, recipes, experience and kitchens. Their generosity of spirit and genuine love of cooking has enriched shows across the state and made this book possible. May it inspire others to discover the joy of cooking and follow in their footsteps.

STATE COMPETITION
Rich Fruit Cake

Tips from the cook

- Start by paying close attention to preparing the cake pan. You must line the pan properly. Make sure the paper has absolutely no creases and fits tightly in the corners.
- Different cooks use different linings for their cake pans, depending on what gets the best results in their oven. Some cooks prefer brown paper. Others use a combination, creating several layers with greaseproof paper or brown paper and alfoil if they want to deflect more heat and slow down the browning process on the outside. Margaret used to line her pan with foil and greaseproof paper, laid in the shape of a 'plus' sign.

Winning the State Rich Fruit Cake Championship is the pinnacle of achievement for show cooks in South Australia. This fiercely contested event draws the ambitions of both experienced and aspiring cooks, and is not easily won.

First, you have to qualify at a regional level in one of eleven semi-finals hosted turnabout by country shows. Even at this level the competition is ferocious, with cooks often travelling from other regions to increase their chances of qualifying. The regional winners then bake new cakes for the state final, which is judged at an open session just before the start of the Royal Adelaide Show.

The championship was the brainchild of highly respected Tanunda show cook, judge, teacher and cookery consultant Margaret Hurst, who wanted to put back something into show cookery because it had given her so much pleasure. Originally from Rowland Flat in the Barossa Valley, Margaret's show cooking career started in Burra when she moved there in 1969 with her husband Neil. She went on to win thousands of prizes and most successful exhibitor awards at shows across the central region of the state and the Mid North, as well as Adelaide. Margaret gave up exhibiting in 1979 to focus on judging, presiding at most shows from Millicent to Wudinna, and in Sydney, Melbourne and Adelaide.

While she treasures all these achievements, the one that stands out in her mind is winning the rich fruit cake class at the Royal Adelaide Show in 1974 against 40 other competitors. The recipe she used became the set recipe for the championship, which was inspired by a similar event in Victoria.

The first final in 1982 was won by the late Iris Redman, from Penola, whose daughter still has a small piece of the winning cake, stored carefully in a glass jar. In the first 26 years there were 16 different winners, including Shirley Harvey, from Strathdownie, just over the South Australian border in western Victoria, who won it six times.

Margaret ran the competition for 25 years before handing over the reins to Margaret Rankin from Wilmington. 'It's been quite a journey for me really,' Margaret Hurst says.

Opposite page: Margaret Hurst **Above:** Professional baker Nick Davey from Orange Spot Bakery judging the 2007 State Rich Fruit Cake Championship **Below:** Finalists in the State Rich Fruit Cake Championship on display at the Royal Adelaide Show (RAHAFSA)

Tips from the judges

- Use a cake pan with square corners and perpendicular sides.
- The judges will be looking for a cake that is cooked properly all the way through and just slightly moist to the touch, rather than dry and crumbly. There should be no damp patches in the centre of the cake.
- The fruit should be evenly distributed through the cake, and the outside an even golden brown colour all over. There should be no sign of shiny, dark or overheated fruit protruding from the surface.
- There should not be any large cracks in the top, or creases or holes in the sides or bottom of the cake. And there should definitely not be any cake rack marks on the bottom of the cake – this alone will be enough to rule it out of contention.
- Do not decorate the cake in any way, even with almonds.
- When the cake is cut there should be a delicious but not overpowering aroma which comes from a perfect blend of fruit, spice, and the sherry or brandy.
- If you are really serious about competing, try to attend an open judging session and listen to the comments and advice of the judges.

Rich Fruit Cake

Recipe

250 g sultanas
250 g raisins
200 g currants
100 g dates
60 g red glace cherries
60 g mixed peel
200 ml sherry or brandy

375 g (2½ cups) plain flour
1 teaspoon baking powder
1 teaspoon mixed spice
250 g butter
250 g dark brown sugar
6 eggs
60 g almonds, chopped

Chop the sultanas, raisins, dates, cherries and mixed peel so that all the fruit is the same size as the currants. Soak the fruit in sherry or brandy overnight.

Preheat the oven to slow (150 °C in a conventional electric oven). Carefully grease and line a deep 19 to 22 cm square cake pan.

Sift together the flour, baking powder and spice.

In a large bowl, cream together the butter and sugar until soft and fluffy, and the sugar is dissolved. Add the eggs one at a time, beating well after each addition. Then add the fruit and flour alternately, and lastly the chopped almonds. Mix thoroughly.

Place the mixture in the prepared pan and bake for about 3 to 3½ hours until golden brown and cooked through.

Tips from the cook

- Make sure you cream the butter and sugar together properly. Undissolved sugar will show up as small white spots on the top of the cake. The mixture should be nice and fluffy, and the sugar completely dissolved.
- Add the eggs one at a time and beat them well between additions. If you add them too quickly, the mixture will curdle and the cake texture will be 'too tight'.
- The most successful show cooks check every single individual piece of dried fruit to make sure it is of good quality.
- The fruit must be even in size, and soaked overnight to plump it up and give it time to absorb the flavour of the brandy or sherry.

Above: An open judging session at the Strathalbyn Show for a regional semifinal of the State Rich Fruit Cake Championship. **Opposite page:** Prize winners in the 2007 State Rich Fruit Cake Championship (HW)

Tips from the cook

- Make sure all the ingredients are evenly distributed through the batter.
- It is important the batter has the right consistency. If it is too 'sloppy' the fruit will sink to the bottom, and if it is too stiff the cake will be dry. A simple test is to pick up a spoonful. The mixture should look silky and drop off the spoon when you flick it gently.
- When you are emptying the mixture into the cake pan, never put the scrapings from the bowl on the top – it can make the cake look patchy. Work the mixture well down into the pan as you go, and smooth it out so the centre is slightly hollow – it will even out as the cake rises and give you a level top.
- Get to know your oven. Every oven is different and knowing how fast it cooks is essential, given that it can be difficult to tell when a fruit cake is cooked to perfection right through. Undercooking is the most common fault – 10 minutes can make the difference between a first prize and nothing at all. If your oven is too hot the top of the cake is likely to crack and the outside will be too dark.
- Bake the cake at least a week before the show to give it time to 'mature'.
- Remove the paper from the cake when it is still warm. If you leave it until later you might get a shiny appearance on the outside.

ADELAIDE

The Royal Adelaide Show is a South Australian institution. Every year a staggering half a million people pass through its gates, making it one of the most successful shows in Australia. The crowds are drawn by a constantly evolving mix of attractions, exhibitions and sideshows, and a rare chance to experience something of the bush, on display in the heart of the city.

The South Australian Agricultural Society was formed in 1839, three years after the arrival of the first European settlers, 'for the advancement of agricultural and pastoral knowledge, and to promote the development of the natural resources of our noble colony'. The society held its first produce show in the grounds of a Grenfell Street hotel in 1840 and the first livestock show followed in Hindley Street in 1843. The society merged with a horticultural organisation in 1844 and staged the genesis of today's show in the same year in Botanic Park, drawing nearly 1200 paying patrons to see John Ridley's historic reaping machine and the first exhibit of local beer.

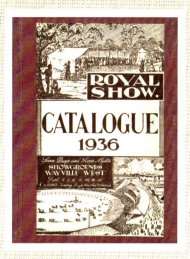

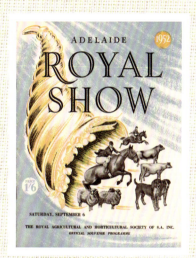

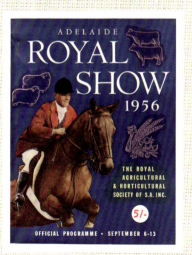

Opposite page, top: Margaret Ennis with her cake entry, 1961 (RAHAFSA)

Opposite page, bottom: Royal Adelaide Show cake display, 1964 (RAHAFSA)

Opposite page, right: Dairy heifer and her young handler at the Royal Adelaide Show (HW)

This page: Royal Adelaide Show programmes (RAHAFSA)

17

Clockwise from top left: Scenes from the Royal Adelaide Show – sideshow rides, the latest fashion in show hats, in the dog pavilion, and a crowd enjoys the entertainment on one of the show's main stages (HW)

Home cooks had to wait until a year after the society moved to its current showground at Wayville in 1925 for the first consolidated set of cookery classes. Twelve exhibitors entered collections of bread, pastries, jams, jellies, scones and small cakes, as well as pound cake, iced fruit cake and plum pudding. They were proudly displayed in a new pavilion on the western side of the showground, which continued to house what became a popular section in its own right until 2008 when the cookery section moved to a higher profile location in the new Goyder Pavilion. By 1935 entrants had the choice of 39 classes, most surprisingly similar to today, including sausage rolls, nut loaf, sponge, sultana cake and cockles, preserved fruits and vegetables.

The show schedule continues to evolve with special sections for professional bakers, commercial cooks making preserves, and novice entrants yet to win a first prize at any Royal Adelaide Show. The open cookery classes are enjoying something of a renaissance too as younger cooks discover baking. Entry numbers increased by more than 30 per cent in the four years to 2007.

Below: Meeting the animals at the alpaca and goat pavilion (HW)

Bottom: Taking in junior art work entries (HW)

ADELAIDE
Chocolate Orange Swirls

Emma Kemp had no idea of the breathtaking audacity of her early attempts to win one of South Australia's most coveted show cooking awards. Something of a celebrity at the Royal Adelaide Show, she won her way into a final of the State Genoa Cake Competition with the first genoa cake she ever made.

The young cook was inspired to start competing at the age of six when she lived at Mil Lel, a few paddocks away from her grandmother Roma Clark. 'I remember when I was little going over and helping her . . . she was one of the best cooks,' says Emma. She later moved to Hahndorf and started entering the Royal Adelaide Show while studying food and hospitality at Heathfield High School.

I didn't realise just how big a deal cooking is at the Adelaide Show, but I got a couple of days off school so that was pretty good. A friend came over and we made these things, and for the first couple of years we were the most successful competitors in the high school section.

At 17 Emma took on the open section and some of the best cooks in the state. 'It was a pretty steep learning curve,' she says. 'But I got friendly with the older ladies who gave me a few tips. They loved it because there was no one else my age entering.' Her efforts met with considerable success, including nine consecutive first prizes for sausage rolls.

In 2007 Emma took a week's holiday from her work as a nurse in the intensive care ward at St Andrew's Hospital and baked steadily for 22 open classes and her biggest challenge to date – the genoa cake finals. She had qualified after winning a semifinal at the Coonalpyn Show with her first attempt at this notoriously difficult cake.

She didn't win the state final but Emma is determined to keep trying. And she enjoys cooking so much there are plans to undertake formal training at some stage and build a part-time career in catering. She already provides catering for family and friends, and was invited to spend a day in the kitchen of the Hilton Hotel with celebrity chef Simon Bryant, trying her hand as a pastry chef. A talented sportswoman, in between her work and cooking, she plays national league level volleyball and is one of the state's best netballers.

Emma invented this biscuit recipe and says it is easy to vary to create all sorts of flavour combinations.

Recipe

375 g (2½ cups) plain flour
100 g (¾ cup) icing sugar
250 g butter
2 tablespoons double cream
2 teaspoons vanilla essence
3 tablespoons cocoa powder
2 teaspoons orange juice
zest of 1 large orange

Sift the flour and icing sugar together, and rub in the butter until the mixture resembles fine breadcrumbs and then starts to come together. Add the cream and vanilla and work into a soft dough.

Divide the dough in half and place in separate bowls. Work the cocoa into one half, and the orange juice and zest into the other half. Lightly knead both lots of dough until they are smooth.

Roll each mixture separately, between two sheets of baking paper, until they are the same thickness (about 4 mm). Remove the baking paper and place one piece of dough on top of the other. Roll them up together quite tightly, lengthwise, to form a log. Wrap the log in plastic cling film and refrigerate until firm (about 30 minutes).

Preheat the oven to moderate (180 °C in a conventional electric oven).

Cut the log into 6 mm thick slices, using a sharp knife. Place them on greased oven trays and bake for 8 to 10 minutes, until just lightly coloured.

Allow to cool slightly on the tray and then remove.

MAKES ABOUT 50 BISCUITS.

Variations
- Use peppermint essence instead of orange juice and zest. You could also add a few drops of green food colouring.
- Substitute the orange juice and zest for 2 teaspoons of strong coffee.

Tips from the cook

- Always use butter, not margarine.
- Pick up the bowl and shake it as if you are panning for gold when you are crumbing the butter and sugar; it helps bring any lumps to the surface. Emma prefers to use her hands to mix the dough but you can use a food processor.
- If the dough has become too warm and soft while you are mixing it, you may need to put it in the fridge for a few minutes before you roll it out so it is easier to handle.
- There is only a fraction of time between a cooked biscuit and a burnt biscuit. Set the oven timer a few minutes short of the recommended cooking time, and then stand by the oven for the last 2 minutes and check them frequently.
- If you take the biscuits off the tray too soon, they will crumble; if you leave them too long, they will stick. Don't use a spatula, and give them a little twist as you lift them so the bottom comes away neatly.

Tips from the judges

- Biscuits must be crisp. They should snap cleanly in half when broken.
- A collection of biscuits must be evenly cooked and uniform in shape and thickness.

Opposite page: Emma Kemp

ADELAIDE
Cockles

Jenny Parish is the only person who has ever won South Australia's two fiercely contested fruit cake competitions in the same year (2002). But her show cooking career had much humbler beginnings; the first things she ever made for competition were simple, old-fashioned cockles, baked for the Coonalpyn Show when she was nine.

Mum had quite often entered cooking and she said to me, 'Why don't you have a go?' So I made cockles, and when we got there they were twice the size of anyone else's. I come from a farm and it's got to be worth eating. I didn't think I should enter them but amazingly enough they won first prize. I got feedback that the size didn't really matter, it was the texture that was the thing.

Jenny gave up show cooking as a teenager and came back to it when she married and moved to Leasingham, where she lives in an old stone house overlooking the family vineyard with her husband Malcolm. She volunteered as a steward at the Clare Show, and then one year took a shot at the local semifinal for the State Rich Fruit Cake Championship.

Tips from the judges

- The cockles should be perfectly round, nicely risen, and with the halves matching exactly.
- Don't be heavy handed with the jam – there should be just enough to make them stick together.
- If you ice them (check the schedules to make sure this is allowed), take the icing out to the edge of the cockle – don't just put a dot in the middle.

'I won it at Clare and I had to go to Adelaide and watch it being judged, and I looked at all the cooking down there and thought I might as well have a go in the open section too.'

Jenny says her husband 'stays away' when she is preparing for the Royal Adelaide Show, where she won the aggregate trophy for cookery in 2006 and 2007. Driven by the challenge, she loves the competition and freely admits she likes to win. 'It's to say I can do it – I can make a better cake than these other ladies,' she says. 'I always played sport and when you play sport you like to win and it's the same with cooking.'

Cockles remain a traditional favourite at many shows and in farmhouse kitchens because they are so easy to make. This is the recipe Jenny used to win her first prize all those years ago.

Recipe

180 g butter
180 g castor sugar
3 eggs (60 g each)
180 g SR flour
90 g cornflour
90 g custard powder
apricot jam

Icing

1 cup icing sugar
squeeze of lemon juice
cold water
desiccated coconut

Preheat the oven to moderate (180 °C in a conventional electric oven).

Cream the butter and the sugar until light and fluffy and the sugar is dissolved. Beat in the eggs, one at a time.

Sift together the flour, cornflour and custard powder. Gradually work the dry ingredients into the butter mixture, using a wooden spoon, until just combined. The mixture should be quite stiff.

Roll teaspoons of the mixture into a ball, and place them on a greased oven tray, about 5 cm apart. Bake for about 10 minutes, until pale golden brown.

Take them off the tray and cool. Match them up with same-sized halves and join them with a smear of apricot jam.

Icing

If desired, combine the icing sugar and lemon juice with a small amount of water to make a smooth icing, and decorate the top of each cockle with icing and a sprinkle of coconut.

MAKES ABOUT 15 COCKLES.

Tips from the cook

- The theory behind this recipe is that you should always use the weight of the eggs in both flour and butter, and in the combination of cornflour and custard powder to get the right consistency. (Author's note: If you are not sure of the accuracy of your scales or the weight of the eggs, weigh them first, make a note of the weight and then match it according to the above formula.)
- If the first batch of cockles spread too much in the oven, the mixture may be too runny – add a little more flour before you bake the next lot.
- Beating the butter and sugar until the sugar is dissolved will improve the final texture.
- The cockles should be no more than 5 cm across when they are cooked, and perhaps a little smaller for shows.
- It's better not to have too much colour – the cockles should be a very light golden brown.
- Jenny prefers to use apricot jam but you can use any type you like.

Opposite page, top: Jenny Parish

ADELAIDE
Tomato Sauce

Tomato sauce recipes are often passed down through the generations but Walter Duncan was not so lucky. The well-known rosarian had to search high and low before he found one that pleased both him and the judges, and he has been applying considerable effort to refining it ever since.

Walter comes from one of South Australia's most prominent show families. His grandfather, Sir Walter Duncan, father, John, and brother, Jock, were all presidents of the Royal Agricultural and Horticultural Show Society (Walter is now treasurer). A leading pastoralist and politician, Sir Walter oversaw the show's move from North Terrace to Wayville where an exhibition hall bearing his name was opened in 1962. Walter recalls 'the thrill of going with him on Sunday to have a look when no one was there. We used to go and see the different exhibitions being set up'. His earliest memories of competing at the show are less pleasant, revolving around the mortifying experience of falling off his pony in front of the member's grandstand at the age of about nine and being carried out of the main arena on a stretcher.

Born to a mother called Rose, Walter has enjoyed growing and exhibiting roses with enormous success for nearly 50 years. He started growing plants and exhibiting them at the show in the 1960s and has chaired the society's horticultural and floricultural committee. He was also responsible for the design of the old rose section

of the Adelaide International Rose Garden. But his pride and joy is The Heritage Garden at his home in the Clare Valley where a small but prolific vegetable garden produces enough tomatoes every year for him to make about 20 litres of sauce.

Walter has been competing in the strongly contested tomato sauce class at the Royal Adelaide Show since the late 1990s, in friendly rivalry with former Supreme Court judge Ted Mulligan. Unhappy with the initial results, Walter went in search of a better recipe and tracked down a preserves judge for advice. She told him to buy a mouli to process the tomatoes and a year later he won the coveted first prize. 'When I found out I rang Ted straight away. He wasn't envious, just totally supportive that one of us had cracked it,' Walter says. Since then Ted has also won, evening the score.

Walter believes the secret to a good sauce lies in reducing the pulp to exactly the right consistency, and striving for 'a bit of a zip' in the flavour. 'It has to have a contrast between the sweetness of the sugar and the bitterness of the vinegar,' he says.

Recipe

10 kg tomatoes (should produce about 9 litres of puree)
For every 9 litres of puree allow:
2.2 litres white vinegar
60 g salt
60–120 g garlic
60 g whole cloves
2 tablespoons dry mustard
3 teaspoons cayenne pepper (optional, or to taste)
60 g allspice (optional, or to taste)
1.5 kg sugar

Process the tomatoes in a mouli or food mill to produce a smooth pulp. Alternatively, remove the skins and seeds from the tomatoes and puree in a blender or processor.

Put the puree into a large saucepan or stockpot. Stir in the vinegar and salt.

Tie the garlic, cloves, mustard, cayenne pepper and allspice into a muslin bag and drop it into the puree mixture.

Boil gently for about 3 hours, stirring occasionally. To test when the sauce is almost ready, drop a small amount onto a cold saucer; there should be little or no watery liquid around the edges.

Now, add the sugar and stir continuously for another 5 to 10 minutes, until the sugar has dissolved and the sauce has thickened a little.

Pour it into sterilised bottles while hot, and seal.

Tips from the cook

- Use a mouli, available from cookware shops, to remove all the seeds and skins and puree the tomatoes.
- Use Roma tomatoes which produce less liquid and more puree to give a more intense flavour, with less reducing time.
- Reduce the sauce to almost 50 per cent to achieve the right intensity of flavour.
- Put the sugar in last so it doesn't caramelise and turn the sauce brown. Judging when the sauce is almost ready so you can add the sugar is one of the 'trickiest' stages.

Tips from the judges

- There should be no skins or seeds in the sauce, and no spices or spots visible.
- The texture should be smooth and flowing, without being too thin, and the colour should be a bright and attractive red.

Opposite page, top: Walter Duncan

ANGASTON
Mumma's Rote Grütze

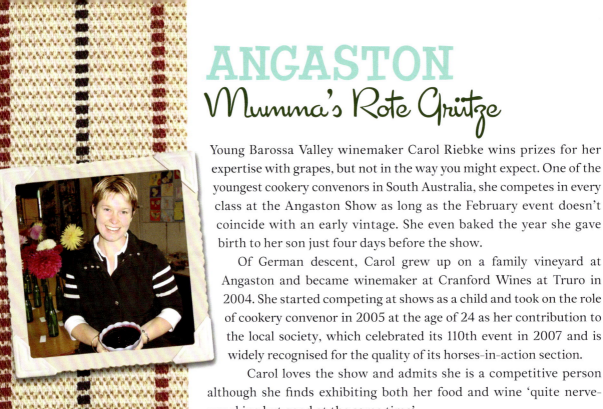

Young Barossa Valley winemaker Carol Riebke wins prizes for her expertise with grapes, but not in the way you might expect. One of the youngest cookery convenors in South Australia, she competes in every class at the Angaston Show as long as the February event doesn't coincide with an early vintage. She even baked the year she gave birth to her son just four days before the show.

Of German descent, Carol grew up on a family vineyard at Angaston and became winemaker at Cranford Wines at Truro in 2004. She started competing at shows as a child and took on the role of cookery convenor in 2005 at the age of 24 as her contribution to the local society, which celebrated its 110th event in 2007 and is widely recognised for the quality of its horses-in-action section.

Carol loves the show and admits she is a competitive person although she finds exhibiting both her food and wine 'quite nerve-wracking but good at the same time'.

It's good to get someone else's opinion on what you are doing, and when you receive first prize or get a grand champion ribbon you know you must be doing the right thing and that spurs you on to keep doing it. I encourage other people to have a go.

Carol couldn't have been more pleased when rote grütze returned to the show schedule in recent years thanks to sponsorship from famous Barossa cook Maggie Beer who wanted to encourage more cooking with grapes. The traditional German dessert is made with sago and grape juice, using shiraz grapes left on the vine until they are very ripe and the natural sugar content is high.

> It's something we had every vintage and as a kid it drove you nuts, but now I appreciate it. I learnt to cook it from my mum and my grandmother [Lorna Doecke], who was a show cook too. Kids love it because it's sweet and has got a lot of flavour – all my nieces go mad for the stuff.

This prizewinning recipe originally came from Carol's grandmother, known as Mumma in the German tradition.

Above: Special display at the Angaston Show, 2007

Opposite page, right: Displays of fruit, vegetables, honey, wine and preserves from Angaston, Barossa Valley, 1914 (SLSA: PRG 280/1/10/465)

Tips from the judges

- Judges usually prefer the natural grape flavours to predominate, so if you are cooking for competition, don't use the cinnamon or lemon.
- Make sure the consistency is neither too runny nor too thick and gluggy.

Opposite page, top: Carol Riebke

Opposite page, left: Angaston show book covers (AAHFSI)

Mumma's Rote Grütze

Recipe

1 kg late-picked shiraz, mataro or grenache grapes
1 cinnamon stick (optional)
1 lemon, sliced (optional)
4 tablespoons sago

Put the grapes in a saucepan with a small amount of water and squeeze them with your hand to extract some juice. Add the cinnamon and lemon if desired, and bring the grapes gently to the boil. Simmer, uncovered, for about 10 minutes.

Let the grapes sit to cool and allow some colour to come out of the skins; the juice should be a rich, dark colour like red wine. Strain the grapes through a sieve, pressing them firmly to extract as much juice as possible.

Return the juice to the saucepan and bring it to the boil. For every cup of juice add 1 tablespoon of sago and keep stirring for about 15 minutes, until the mixture thickens and the sago is clear.

Pour the rote grütze into a bowl or storage container and chill in the fridge until set.

Serve it warm or cold, with ice-cream or cream.

Tips from the cook

- You can use commercial grape juice instead of grapes to make your own, but it won't taste the same.
- Wine grapes are best, not table grapes; shiraz and mataro are the preferred varieties, although some people use grenache.
- The fruit needs to be very ripe so it contains enough natural sugar and generates enough colour from the skin of the grapes.
- 1 kilogram of grapes should produce about 1 litre of juice.
- Carol does not use cinnamon or lemon in her version, and she doesn't add any sugar. She also prefers not to dilute the flavour by adding large amounts of water to cook the grapes.
- The trick to achieving the right consistency lies in making sure you keep stirring the mixture once the sago is added so it doesn't stick together.
- The flavour is best when you serve it warm, with a little cream.

Opposite page: Judging cakes at the 2007 Angaston Show

BALAKLAVA
Mango Diabetic Fruit Cake

Doris Wandel was a formidable show cook who often set the standard for other competitors. Doris died unexpectedly in January 2007 at the age of 81, after more than 50 years competing and judging at shows from Clare to Renmark and Adelaide. Originally from the Barossa Valley, she spent most of her life on a farm near Balaklava with Clarrie, her husband of 60 years.

'She did it for the love of cooking,' says daughter Christine Burford who draws on her mother's memory for inspiration in her own efforts as a show cook and judge.

It's probably in our genes. It came from her mum to her. Mum used to always say there was no way in the world she would take it on but she went to the Adelaide Show once and [after looking at the entries] thought she would have a go. It finished up she was doing everything right through the whole book. I can remember as a child, we used to start at Gawler and then end up at Clare in the middle of October. Nearly every week there was a show.

Doris always encouraged her daughter not to give up if she didn't win a prize, and displayed equal tenacity herself. She kept a record of failures as well as successes so she could work on improving her skills leading up to the next show. 'The main lesson she taught me was don't throw the towel in when you have a failure. She always told me if it doesn't turn out have another go.'

Christine is not sure of the origins of this fruit cake recipe but says her mother used it for many years after becoming a diabetic in later life. A trophy is given in her honour for the best diabetic fruit cake entered in the Balaklava Show, a spring event which draws about 2000 people. The show began in 1875 and, apart from three years during World War II, has been held every year since. Horses-in-action are a major feature, along with an entertainment marquee that showcases local talent.

Above: Doris Wandel, her husband Clarrie and daughter Christine Burford, 1997 (N/AA)
Opposite page: Doris Wandel, 1994 (N/AA)

Tips from the judges
- The cake should be nice and moist.
- Sinking in the centre or a heavy texture means the oven was probably too cool or the cake isn't cooked enough.

Recipe

- 425 g tin mango slices in natural juice, drained, juice reserved
- 500 g mixed fruit
- ½ cup water
- 1½ cups SR flour
- 1½ teaspoons bicarbonate of soda
- 2 eggs, beaten

Preheat the oven to slow (160 °C in a conventional electric oven). Grease and line the bottom of either a loaf pan or a 20 cm round cake pan.

Chop the mango. Put it in a large saucepan with the juice, mixed fruit and water. Bring to the boil, and boil for 1 minute.

Cool the mixture for 10 minutes or so. Sift together the flour and soda. Stir it into the fruit mixture with the beaten eggs.

Mix well and pour into the prepared pan. Bake for 1 hour.

Tips from the cook's family

- Make sure you cool the fruit and water before adding the dry ingredients and eggs, so the eggs don't start cooking as you stir them in.
- Check the cake after it has been in the oven for about 45 minutes – if it is browning too quickly, cover the top with brown paper or alfoil.

BORDERTOWN
Eggplant and Chilli Chutney

People in the Bordertown area still talk about Ralph Adams and the wonderful sauces, chutneys, relishes and jams he made using fruit and vegetables from his own garden and orchard.

Ralph died in a home accident in 2003. He had already organised his entries for the local show, so the society asked his family to go ahead and enter them as a special tribute. 'He had his entries ready to go. They were in the cellar and everything was written up,' recalls daughter Prue Clark.

Ralph started showing in his seventies, after winding back the amount of time he spent working the family farm to care for his ill wife. A person who liked to be active, he also spent more time in the garden nurturing a vast array of vegetables and expanding the household orchard. Preserving the excess fruits of his labour seemed a logical next step. He started by making tomato sauce from Roma tomatoes frozen until winter when he had more time and it was cooler to work in the kitchen.

He loved making his sauce on the same old Rayburn slow combustion stove which had kept the Greenways kitchen warm for more than 40 years. As Dad increased his produce, so too increased his thirst for new recipes . . . If he couldn't find a recipe he invented one.

Prue is certain her father's self-sufficiency came from helping his mother, who was blind. The family moved quite a few times during the Depression; he acted as her eyes for the first few weeks in each new location and helped out in the kitchen.

Prue remembers her father as a 'gentle, precious soul' who thoroughly enjoyed the admiration his cooking endeavours brought him. His success was often the talking point at the Bordertown Spring Festival, the town's annual show, which celebrated its 130th anniversary in 2007. Today a combination of traditional and contemporary attractions, the event started as a ploughing match and horse show offering a lucrative £60 in prize money. A prize of 50 guineas for the best wheat was added in 1883, reflecting the agricultural achievements of farmers in 'the good country'.

Recipe

small piece of ginger root
2 red chillies
1 tablespoon curry powder
600 ml cider vinegar
2 or 3 medium red capsicums, chopped finely
2 large green apples, peeled and chopped finely
250 g onions, chopped finely
2 cloves garlic, sliced and crushed
600 ml water
2 medium eggplants, peeled and chopped into pieces about 1 cm square
185 g seeded raisins
375 g light brown sugar
1 teaspoon salt

Pound the ginger lightly to bruise. Split the chillies in half lengthwise, and then cut in halves again cross ways. Tie the ginger and chillies together in a muslin bag.

Mix the curry powder with a little of the vinegar to form a smooth paste.

Put the capsicum, apples and onions in large a pan or stockpot with the garlic, vinegar and water. Simmer until soft.

Add the eggplant, raisins, muslin bag, sugar and salt. Stir in the curry paste. Simmer uncovered for about 1 to $1^1/_2$ hours, stirring occasionally, until thick.

Remove the muslin bag. Bottle and seal while hot.

Tips from the cook's family

- Ralph liked to remove the seeds from the chilli, which he said reduced the heat. Prue likes to leave them in.
- If you don't have a muslin bag, use a small piece of loosely woven fabric, tied with butcher's twine.
- If the raisins are large, cut them in half.

Tips from the judges

- A bright colour and plenty of flavour without being too hot are the key attributes of a prizewinning chutney.
- Make sure the vegetables and fruits are cut evenly.

Above: Bordertown showground gates **Opposite page:** Ralph Adams (PC)

Above: Wally Cook shearing an alpaca at the Bordertown Spring Festival (TBC)

BURRA
Lemon Slice

The first show at Burra was most likely held in 1877, just a few weeks before the great Burra Burra Copper Mine finally ceased operations. Although the catalogue of competitive classes were limited and the weather drizzly, a large crowd gathered in the town's old smelting works to enjoy the spectacle.

The organising society went into recess for nine years in the late 19th century, but came back stronger than ever, hosting a special sheep show in 1916 where livestock with an estimated market value of £13,000 were put on display. The district's reputation as one of the world's most important stud sheep centres continues to be reflected in today's program, with special events like the Copper Shears shearing competition.

Lining up for many years in classes for sheep and wool were Hazel and Rex Stockman and their Springvale Merino Stud. Hazel can remember missing only one Burra show since she was a child – ironically the year she and Rex were made life members. 'Since I was a baby, I had never missed a show,' she says, reflecting on her childhood at nearby World's End. 'I can remember going and picking sheaves of wheat to bring in and I remember we used to exhibit pork sausages.'

Hazel first entered the show in her own right soon after she was married. She quickly became 'hooked', and the passion for competing at shows grew until the whole family was involved, preparing hundreds of entries for everything from sheep and wool to cooking and needlework. 'We had four kids early in our married years and they all exhibited . . . Where we lived I had two ovens which made it easy to get through a lot of things in a short time.'

Hazel gradually worked her way through every cookery class in the show book, volunteered as a steward, and went on to become a judge for both cookery and handicrafts. This lemon slice recipe usually formed part of a collection of three she prepared for the uncooked slice class. Hazel is not certain of its origins but she tends to use tried-and-true recipes for competition. 'I am a great person for looking at a recipe, trying it and if it works the first time I will keep it, otherwise it goes out. I love experimenting with new things.'

Tips from the cook

- If you intend to use this slice for a show collection, match it with slices that have contrasting and bold colours, like a jelly slice topped with lime jelly and the red of a cherry slice. 'Eye appeal is so important. I was always a great colour coordinator so it looked nice on the plate,' Hazel says.
- To get the icing nice and smooth, use a knife dipped in hot water.

Tips from the judges

- Make sure the icing is thin, smooth and comes sharply to the edge of the slice.

Recipe

125 g butter
200 ml sweetened condensed milk
1 (250 g) packet Marie biscuits (or similar), crushed
$3/4$ cup desiccated coconut

rind of 1 lemon
desiccated coconut, extra

Lemon icing

$1^{1}/_{2}$ cups icing sugar
juice of 1 lemon
yellow food colouring

Melt the butter in a large saucepan, remove from the heat and add the condensed milk. Stir in the remaining ingredients. Press the mixture into a Swiss roll pan (25 cm by 30 cm) and refrigerate. When set, top the slice with the icing and sprinkle it with the extra coconut.

Lemon icing

Combine the icing sugar, lemon juice and enough food colouring to achieve your preferred colour.

Opposite page, top: Hazel Stockman
Right: Sheep shed at Burra showground
Far right: Admission gateway at Burra showground

CALLINGTON
Curried Zucchini Relish

At a time when many country shows were struggling to continue, the historic town of Callington took a bold step and created a new one. Strongly supported by 350 or so residents, the surrounding farming community and a host of businesses, the show has become a highlight of the town's calendar since it started in 2002 as the Callington Miner's Fair.

The event was initially organised to celebrate the rich mining history of the district, which became the site of Australia's first commercially successful copper smelter in 1848. Set on the banks of the Bremer River, between Mount Barker and Murray Bridge, Callington sprang into life after a carrier noticed signs of copper when some stone was crushed by the wheel of his bullock dray. At one time the district had five mines but keeping the shafts free of water proved a constant challenge.

Among regular competitors who contest the Callington Show's cookery and preserves classes every October is Cherrol Wundersitz. Cherrol lives just outside the town on a cereal and sheep property, with her husband Clive. Although her daughter, Michelle Green, competes at the Royal Adelaide Show in decorated cake classes, Cherrol only took up show cooking when the Callington event started and has never really been interested in competing anywhere else.

She tries to enter something different every year and has won championship ribbons and first prizes for a range of her favourite

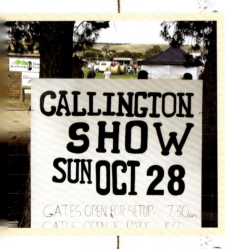

recipes. While Cherrol is best known for her slices and cakes, judges find her curried zucchini relish hard to resist too. She can't remember the recipe's origins, but she has been making it for many years using fresh vegetables from her garden and happily shares jars with family and visitors. It's easy to make. Try it with a slab of vintage cheddar, or alongside some cold roast lamb.

Recipe

500 g zucchini, chopped finely
1 green capsicum, chopped finely
1 red capsicum, chopped finely
3 onions, chopped finely
2 sticks celery, chopped finely
$\frac{1}{4}$ cup salt
$1\frac{1}{2}$ cups white vinegar
1 kg tomatoes, peeled and chopped
2 cups sugar
2 heaped tablespoons plain flour
2 level tablespoons dry mustard
2 heaped tablespoons curry powder
$\frac{1}{4}$ cup water

Place the zucchini, green and red capsicum, onions and celery in a bowl. Sprinkle the vegetables with the salt and add enough cold water to cover. Leave overnight.

Next day drain and rinse the vegetables with cold water. Place them in a large pot with the vinegar and bring to the boil. Boil for 10 minutes.

Add the tomatoes and simmer for another 5 minutes.

Add the sugar and stir the mixture until it returns to the boil.

Blend the flour, mustard, curry powder and water into a smooth paste. Add to the pot, and stir in thoroughly. Boil for another 5 minutes.

Bottle and seal the relish while hot, in sterilised jars.

Tips from the cook

- Use an English-style dry mustard.
- You might like to add more mustard if you want a hotter relish.

Tips from the judges

- Cut all the vegetables into even-sized pieces. Smaller pieces are likely to appeal to most judges, while you might prefer a chunkier version to serve at home.

Opposite page, top: Cherrol Wundersitz
Opposite page, bottom right: Junior wheelbarrow race at the Callington Show
Bottom left: Senior wheelbarrow race at the Callington Show

CLARE
Chocolate Crackles

Take four children, add flour, eggs, milk, butter, cocoa powder and quite a bit of stirring, and you are likely to have chaos on a grand scale. Heather Lymburn wouldn't have it any other way; she is the mother of four passionate young cooks who choose to spend their spring school holidays at home in the kitchen cooking up a storm for the Clare Show.

Amy, Isobel, Emily and Thomas have a clutch of ribbons and prize cards for their jubilee cake, rock buns, decorated novelty cakes and – the ultimate for many junior cooks – chocolate crackles. 'It's great because even at a very young age, they are quite competent cooks,' Heather says. 'They have not been terribly interested in sports . . . but they excel at this and it's really rewarding for them. Cooking is something not valued as much as sport in society today but it's an important skill to have.'

To keep a lid on the chaos, Heather divides the kitchen into separate work areas, and helps negotiate oven space and access to the equipment. Until recent years, she also made a ruling that only one child could enter any given class, to avoid in-family competition. But the kids have proven they are friendly rivals so she now lets them enter as many as they like. In 2007, there was at least one Lymburn family entry in every junior class of the Clare Show, one of the largest two-day country shows in the state, which celebrated its 140th show in 2004 and draws more than 5000 exhibitors and about 30,000 patrons.

The Lymburns tend to rely on the tried-and-true *Green and Gold Cookery Book* for inspiration, but their chocolate crackles recipe is another matter. Not happy with the approach suggested in the traditional recipe often found on the back of cereal packets, they have devised their own 'secret' combination which has proven a winner both at home and in competition. It uses more cereal and less copha than normally recommended.

Above: Amy, Isobel, Emily and Thomas Lymburn

Opposite page, top: Setting up an indoor display of local produce at the Clare Show, c. 1940. In the foreground are members of the Knapstein family from Stanley Winery (NTSA, Clare district)

Opposite page, bottom: Show day at Clare, 1926 (SLSA: B 28964/1)

Tips from the judges

- The judges are looking for neatness so be careful how you put the mixture into the patty pans.
- The rice cereal should be evenly coated with the copha mixture.
- Chocolate crackles must be shown in the patty pans in which they are made.

Tips from the cooks

- Leave the mixture in the bowl until it starts to set so the chocolate coating doesn't settle in the bottom of the patty pans. It will start to lose its glossy appearance when it is ready.
- The Lymburns prefer not to decorate their chocolate crackles for competition.

Recipe

200 g copha
6 cups rice cereal
1 cup icing sugar, sifted
3 tablespoons cocoa powder, sifted
1 cup desiccated coconut

Melt the copha in a microwave oven.

In a large bowl, mix together the cereal, icing sugar, cocoa and coconut. Pour in the melted copha and stir until well combined.

Let the mixture stand and start to set a little before spooning it into small patty pans.

MAKES ABOUT 30 CHOCOLATE CRACKLES.

Above: Emily, Amy, Thomas and Isobel Lymburn making chocolate crackles

Opposite page, left: Judging the home brew (TFr)

Opposite page, right: Tom Broad of Burra with his champion modern game bantam at the 2007 Clare Show (NA)

CLEVE
Zucchini, Apple and Carrot Muffins

Hannah Stringer learnt to cook from her grandmother, Noreen Hannemann. 'My Nanna has all my show books from the time I started, and she taught me everything I know,' recalls Hannah, who entered her first show at about the age of seven. 'I remember making some decorated biscuits. They were jam biscuits with beautiful pink icing. I made them from scratch and they became a family favourite.'

Noreen is a show cook too and Hannah's fondest memories revolve around the two of them working side by side in her grandmother's kitchen preparing their entries.

I remember taking it all down to the showgrounds, and the excitement of going into the hall [after judging] and looking through all the awards with Mum and Nanna; I felt very proud to have two great role models to work from. It was the process that I loved – spending time with Nanna and learning from her all the show tricks that she had learnt. I am still learning the trickier things. I just want to be as good as her . . . Cooking is an art.

Studying early childhood education at university in Adelaide, Hannah hopes one day she, like her Nanna, can pass on her skills and passion for cooking to her own children and grandchildren. Meanwhile, she has chosen to share a favourite recipe for muffins. Noreen donates a special prize for the junior muffin class at the Cleve Show, where the schedule has changed over the years to reflect contemporary trends in the kitchen. The inaugural event in 1909 rewarded makers of the best pound and seed cakes, tarts or cheesecakes, meat pies and 'collection cookery'. By the time the 50th show came around in 1958 the preserves section included, unusually, preserved mushrooms; and cookery classes featured such delicacies as Napoleon cake and sponge lilies which have virtually disappeared from today's cookery schedules.

Tips from the cook

- Make sure the spices are well mixed.
- Hannah prefers to use Granny Smith apples and canola oil, but any light-flavoured oil is fine.
- Do not overwork the mixture or the muffins will be chewy.
- Let the muffins sit before you remove them from the pan to stop them going flat.
- The mixture needs to fill the pan to make a good-sized muffin.

Tips from the judges

- Muffins should be cooked in tins, not patty pans.
- If baked too slowly, muffins will peak and leave a hollow around the edge. In too hot an oven they will crack and become unsymmetrical.
- They should have firm sides and rounded tops, and be neat and clean with no loose crumbs.

Recipe

2 cups plain flour
2 teaspoons bicarbonate of soda
2 teaspoons cinnamon
$1/8$ teaspoon nutmeg
$1/8$ teaspoon ginger
$1/8$ teaspoon allspice
$1/2$ teaspoon salt
1 cup brown sugar, firmly packed
2 medium zucchinis, grated
1 apple, cored and grated coarsely
1 medium carrot, grated (optional)
$1/2$ cup chopped almonds
3 eggs
1 cup oil
2 teaspoons vanilla essence

Preheat the oven to moderate (180 °C in a conventional electric oven). Grease a medium-sized ($1/2$ cup) muffin pan.

Sift together into a large bowl the flour, soda, cinnamon, nutmeg, ginger, allspice and salt. Add the sugar and mix well. Stir in the zucchini, apple, carrot and almonds.

In a separate bowl, beat together the eggs, oil and vanilla. Stir this egg mixture into the flour mixture until the batter is just combined.

Spoon the mixture into pre-greased muffin pans, filling to the top. Bake for 20 minutes or until golden brown. Leave the muffins in the tray for 5 minutes before removing them from the pan and placing them on a rack to cool.

MAKES 14 MEDIUM-SIZED MUFFINS.

Opposite page, top: Hannah Stringer

Opposite page, bottom: Teams of four horses competing at Cleve Show, c. 1925 (SLSA: B 27944)

COONALPYN
Homemade Bread

Mavis Klitscher has entered at least one indoor class at the Coonalpyn Show every year since it started. Originally from Yorke Peninsula, she came to the district as a young girl, married a local farmer and stayed. Her father, Otto Jericho, served as inaugural president of the Coonalpyn and District Agricultural and Horticultural Society when it was formed in 1945 by a community keen to demonstrate that farms in the surrounding Ninety Mile Desert were capable of growing quality produce and helping in the effort to feed a war-ravaged world.

The first 'show' was organised a year before by the local Agricultural Bureau. While it mainly took the form of on-farm visits to inspect pastures and machinery, the day also brought together women of the district to display their skills in cooking, home produce and flower arranging. The first proper show featured fourteen sections, horse racing, sports and athletic competitions. Indoor displays were held under the awnings of a hired marquee. This was replaced by a simple iron-clad building, dismantled and moved each year from the local grain-handling facility.

Actively supported by a vibrant local community, the Coonalpyn Show continues to thrive with a popular tractor-pull drawing extra crowds every second year. Indoors, special prizes reward convenors and stewards in charge of the best-presented section, with produce lovingly showcased on long tables and tiered stands.

Until recently the entries usually included breads and rolls made by Mavis, who competed at several shows across the region. She was inspired by Peter Van the Bread Man after attending a baking demonstration in Adelaide. Mavis made bread regularly for her own family, as well as German apple yeast cake, fruit buns, donuts and fresh bread rolls. Her daughter Lynette also remembered the joy of being able to eat prizewinning cakes, sausage rolls and pikelets brought home after judging.

While her health no longer allows her to spend hours on her feet cooking, Mavis still organises flowers from her garden for the Cut Flowers section. 'We have got the show in our blood,' she says.

Recipe

1 kg bread flour
2 teaspoons salt
2 dessertspoons dry yeast*
1 dessertspoon bread improver*
600 ml warm water

*the quantity used per kilogram of flour may vary depending on brand. Check the packet for preferred amounts.

Place a rack in the middle of the oven and preheat the oven to 65 °C.

Mix together all the ingredients and knead for 5 minutes. Cover with a tea towel and stand in the oven for 15 minutes or until double in size.

Remove the dough from the oven, punch down and knead for several more minutes until smooth and elastic.

Divide the dough in half and place it in two bread tins. Cover the tins with a tea towel and place them back in the oven to rise for another 20 minutes.

Take the dough out of the oven and stand, covered, in a warm place. Set the oven to hot (220 °C in a conventional oven) and wait for about 10 minutes. Put the bread in the oven and bake for 20 minutes.

Tips from the cook

- The most important element is good quality bread flour.
- Make sure the water is warm but not too hot or it will kill the yeast.
- Keep the dough warm. Warm the bowl you use to mix the dough, and even have the flour warm too. 'Once you start working it, don't stop for anything,' says Mavis.

Tips from the judges

- The judges will be looking for a well-shaped loaf, with neat and clean sides and a smooth, well-rounded top. The loaf should make a hollow sound when tapped on the base.
- The bread should have a sweet, yeasty aroma and a fine, even texture.

Opposite page, top: Mavis Klitscher (MK)

Left: Preserves section entries on display at the Coonalpyn Show

CRYSTAL BROOK
Coffee Kisses

Mavis Crawford started show cooking in about 1945, spurred on by the words of her recently acquired mother-in-law: 'you will never be as good a cook as me.' During more than 50 years of competing, Mavis proved her wrong time and again, winning 28 prizes with 30 entries at one show alone. She even became a judge, on one memorable occasion travelling to Hobart to assess entries in a Giant Home Cooking Contest.

'Mum was always a good cook and I was always interested in cooking and making up my own recipes,' she says, recalling that her mother earnt money selling homemade pasties to workers on the Whyalla pipeline for five pence each.

Mavis used to set aside one day a week for baking, using milk, cream, butter and eggs from the farm, and chopped her own wood for the stove to make sure it was 'just right'. The tempo would increase dramatically come showtime as she worked over many days, covering a bed in the spare room with her entries. 'The highlight was that the family backed me. They all encouraged me to do it,' she says.

Cookery competitions formed no part of the first show at Crystal Brook – a ploughing match and horse show held on a fine August day in 1874. But in what seems to be a relatively rare occurrence, women did at least get a mention in the *Chronicle's* report of the occasion. 'It would have done any bachelors heart good to see the wagon load of blooming farmers daughters arrayed in their holiday attire – and looking the very picture of health and beauty!' the correspondent

wrote. By 1910, the event was drawing more than 8000 patrons. Organised by the North Western Agricultural Society, the show continues to have a reputation for innovation, and the society puts a great deal of effort into encouraging young exhibitors, particularly in the cookery section.

Taken from an old cookbook that came with one of her first electric stoves, Mavis says these coffee kisses were always popular when she made them for local gatherings. And they are quick and easy too.

Recipe

185 g (1¼ cups) SR flour
pinch of salt
90 g butter
60 g (¼ cup) castor sugar

1 egg
1 dessertspoon coffee essence
½ teaspoon vanilla essence
jam or icing

Preheat the oven to moderately hot (200 °C in a conventional electric oven).

Sift together the flour and salt. Cream the butter and sugar in a small bowl until light and fluffy.

In a separate bowl, beat the egg, then add the coffee and vanilla. Gradually add the egg mixture to the butter and sugar. Stir in the flour to make a stiff consistency.

When the dough is well mixed, use a teaspoon to drop it on a greased oven tray. Bake for 8–10 minutes.

Place on a cake rack to cool. When cold, join two halves together with jam or icing. Sprinkle the top with a little icing sugar.

MAKES ABOUT 12 COMPLETED KISSES.

Tips from the cook

- Try using a bit less sugar, which can also help make the texture finer for showing.
- Mavis likes joining them with strawberry jam.
- If you are using salted butter you might not need to add extra salt.
- You don't have to use castor sugar in this recipe, ordinary white sugar will do.

Tips from the judges

- The kisses should be uniform in size and shape, slightly domed, with the pairs matching exactly.
- The layer of filling must be even and the finish smooth, with no loose flour.

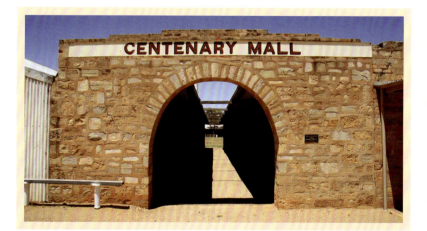

Opposite page, top: Mavis Crawford and cookery section convenor Julie Price

Opposite page, bottom right: Visitors inspecting a display of farm machinery at an agricultural show held at Crystal Brook, 1915 (SLSA: PRG 280/1/27/190)

Left: Centenary Mall, Crystal Brook showground

CUMMINS
Quince Jelly

Tucked away behind Jan Nitschke's modest house in the centre of Cummins is a garden that reflects her true passion in life. The rambling series of 'garden rooms' are home to a remarkable collection of flowers, shrubs, vegetables, fruit and nut trees and grape vines. Among them is an unusual grape variety grown from a cutting said to have been brought back from Gallipoli by a local soldier. 'When the grapes are ripe you can go down in the garden and smell this beautiful perfume,' Jan says. 'It's a little black grape and it tastes like a liqueur. Our family loves it.'

An experienced show cook and keen competitor, Jan spent her childhood being 'dragged' around shows by her mother who also competed and judged. Jan followed in her footsteps when she married and moved to Port Pirie, entering classes at the nearby Crystal Brook show. Describing herself as 'extremely lucky', she has had considerable success over the years, winning six trophies at one show alone. 'I started pretty young and it's been one of my great interests over the years . . . but you have to be a little mad,' she admits. Convenor of the jams and pickles section at Cummins for more than fifteen years, she doesn't enter as much these days but encourages others to take up the challenge and 'help make a show of it'.

Competition in the indoor section is still keen at the event which started in 1911. A special effort is made to entice young people from the local school to participate, with a regional trophy going to the school with the highest amount of entries based on percentage of pupils. A growing indoor trade section, local musicians, entertainers from Adelaide, and a sit-down lunch catered by show volunteers round out the day.

Jan says jellies are pretty easy to make. This recipe is a hand-me-down from her mother.

Tips from the cook

- You may need to adjust the amount of water. The aim is to make sure the fruit is covered.
- Do not stir the fruit while you are cooking it – you will end up with impurities in the juice.
- Try using jam-setting sugar, available from most supermarkets, which contains pectin. Once you have added the sugar, do not allow the jelly to re-boil until it is completely dissolved.
- If you don't have a suitable cloth for the draining process, try using a clean Chux cloth.
- To test whether the jelly is set, put a small amount on a cold plate. It is ready when a skin forms or it starts to gel.

Recipe

6 medium-sized quinces   sugar (about 3 cups)
7 cups water

Wash the quinces well to remove any fluff on the skin, and rub dry with a towel. Place them in a pan with the water. Put the lid on and simmer very gently for 3 to 4 hours until the fruit is very tender and a rich red colour.

Line a large colander or sieve with muslin or a loose-weave cloth. Place it over a large bowl and pour in the contents of the pan. Do not touch or press the fruit – this will add impurities to the jelly and cause it to go cloudy. Leave it to drain overnight, or for at least 2 hours, until all the juice has dripped through.

Measure the juice and pour it into a saucepan. To every cup of juice add 1 cup of sugar. Bring slowly to the boil, stirring until the sugar is completely dissolved. Boil rapidly until set (about 10 minutes depending on pectin levels and based on about 1 litre of jelly).

Carefully pour the jelly into jars, and use a skewer to bring any bubbles to the surface. Fill the jar right to the top, which allows for shrinkage, and leave to set. Seal with cellophane and a rubber band.

Tips from the judges

- Be careful to use the correct amount of sugar to avoid toughness or thinness.
- Pour boiling water through the cloth before you start straining the fruit. For the best results, try suspending the fruit from the legs of an upturned stool or chair.
- Using a spoon, remove any scum from the top of the jelly before you start bottling it.
- Make sure you exhibit the correct number and size of jars, sealed according to the requirements of the show schedule. If there are no specific instructions the best-sized jar is 500 g. Jellies are usually sealed with cellophane although screw tops can also be used.
- Make sure the jars are clean and shiny, with no finger marks, and that the label is centred properly.
- Jellies should be clear and bright, without sediment, cloudiness or air bubbles.
- Do not present jellies that have been judged at another show. Any attempts to re-smooth the surface will lose points.

Opposite page, top: Jan Nitschke

Opposite page, bottom: Cummins show book cover, 1958 (CAHSI)

Above: Cummins show book cover, 1961 (CAHSI)

Left: Sheep pens at the Cummins showground

EUDUNDA
Honey Biscuits

Cookery was not on the programme when 600 people gathered in 'admirable' weather for the first livestock show and ploughing match at Eudunda. Four years later, in 1900, German cake, pickles and jam lined up alongside best-ironed white shirts and crocheted petticoats in the 'Miscellaneous Section'.

By 1929 cookery was holding its own, with more than 30 entries in one cake class alone. The 1931 event featured some innovative classes – prizes for the best invalid's tray and father's luncheon. 'The ladies of the Eudunda District certainly can cook,' reported the *Eudunda Courier*. The show lapsed for a year during World War II, only to bounce back in 1941 as the Eudunda Patriotic Show. Cooking entries suffered because of a shortage of rationed ingredients such as sugar, but the event raised a healthy sum for wartime causes.

Special trains brought people from Adelaide and Morgan for many years to what became one of the state's most successful agricultural shows, reflecting a rich farming heritage made familiar through the books of famous local author, Colin Thiele.

The district's German heritage also continues to influence the cookery and preserves classes. Lining up alongside bright jars of pickles, bottled fruit and sprawling German yeast cakes are the less ostentatious but equally traditional honey biscuits. And more often than not, claiming first prize in this class is Ora Jenke.

Ora started competing in 1961 after she married; her mother-in-law was a show cook and suggested she enter. 'That first year I did get a few prizes and it encouraged me,' Ora says. She went on to serve as a steward for 25 years, and was convenor of the cookery section for many years, receiving a special trophy from the Northern Shows Association for her contribution.

Ora often uses locally produced honey for her biscuits which she cooks regularly as a fundraiser for the Adelaide Women's and Children's Hospital. The recipe is adapted from one provided for volunteers from the Lutheran Women of South Australia.

Top: Ora Jenke **Left:** Eudunda show book cover, 1901 (EDAHSI)

Opposite page, top: Mark Eckermann and son William with prizewinning cow Pella Golden Beauty and daughter at the 1964 show (EDAHSI) **Opposite page, bottom:** Mona Schiller, Olga Noll, Jean Schmidt, Una Sachse, Yvonne Sachse and Pat Sachse at the 1952 Eudunda Show (EDAHSI)

Recipe

185 g (3/4 cup) sugar
3/4 cup honey
30 ml boiling water
2 level teaspoons bicarbonate of soda (dissolved in the water)
1 egg, beaten
plain flour, at least 500 g (3 cups)
ground ginger (at least 1/2 teaspoon)
a small pinch of salt

Combine the sugar, honey, water and soda in a saucepan. Put the saucepan on a warm heat and stir the mixture continuously until the sugar starts to dissolve.

Let it cool a little, and then add the egg and mix thoroughly. Transfer the mixture to a large bowl.

Sift together the flour, ginger and salt. Add gradually to the mixture, using a knife or fork to form a very stiff dough. Refrigerate the dough for at least 1 hour.

Preheat the oven to moderate (190 °C in a conventional electric oven).

Roll the dough out on a well-floured board to a thickness of about 5 mm and cut into desired shapes.

Place on lightly greased oven trays and bake for about 10 minutes, until golden.

Leave them on the tray for a couple of minutes before moving them to a flat surface to cool. Once the biscuits are cool, store them in an airtight container.

MAKES ABOUT 120 SMALL BISCUITS.

Tips from the cook

- Vary the amount of spice in these biscuits according to personal taste.
- The quantity given for flour is approximate – the idea is to add enough flour to make very stiff dough. This may vary depending on the size eggs you use.
- Refrigerating the dough makes it easier to roll. You can keep the dough in the fridge until the next day as long as it is well wrapped.
- These biscuits are delicious iced, or try glazing them with a sugar syrup and sprinkling them with hundreds and thousands before baking.

Opposite page, top left and right: Judging preserves at the Eudunda Show **Opposite page, right:** The cookery and preserves section at the Eudunda Show **Opposite page, bottom:** Recording competition results

Tips from the judges

- Make sure there is no flour on the biscuits and no rack marks.
- The biscuits should be cut neatly and cooked so they are even in colour.
- They need to break easily when the judge goes to snap them.

GAWLER
Rock Buns

More than 200 volunteers lend their time and energy to stage the impressive two-day show at Gawler every spring. Among them is Kath Palamountain, who has been convenor of the cookery section since 1982, having first served her apprenticeship as a steward and competitor.

Kath baked her first cakes for competition in 1964. 'I ended up winning a prize . . . I think it was a boiled fruit cake and that got me started,' she says. Originally from Mallala, she was a farmer's daughter and an 'outside girl' not much into cooking. But she learnt by trial and error and has had considerable success over the years, particularly with rock buns – a popular class at Gawler.

The Gawler Show attracts about 400 cooking entries, making it one of the largest cookery sections in the state. More than 5000 entries are usually received across the show, which draws up to 30,000 patrons every year, with strong competition in beef cattle and horse events as well as the indoor sections, and a large number of trade displays.

The local society was formed in 1854 to promote agriculture and horticulture, and initially focused on holding regular lectures by farming experts and running ploughing matches. The first show was staged in February 1856, drawing settlers from miles around who were 'delighted with the display of fruit which comprised as fine

Opposite page, top: Kath Palamountain

Opposite page, bottom: Band playing on the arena (GAHFSI)

Bottom: Stock parading in the ring during an agricultural show held at Gawler, 1923 (SLSA: PRG 280/1/41/89)

Left: Sheep exhibitors at the Gawler Show (GAHFSI)

Below: Entries in fruit classes (GAHFSI)

Top left: Preserves section entries (GAHFSI)

Top right: Tractors on show (GAHFSI)

Above, left and right: Sideshow alley (GAHFSI)

Right: Beef cattle judging (GAHFSI)

specimens of garden produce as any district in the country could have exhibited', according to a report in the *South Australian Register*. Gawler celebrated its 150th show in 2006.

Recipe

2 heaped cups SR flour, sifted
3/4 cup sugar
1 teaspoon mixed spice (optional)
lemon juice (generous squeeze from half a lemon)
125 g butter
2 eggs
1/2 cup milk
lemon essence (a few drops)
250 g mixed fruit

Preheat the oven to moderate (180 °C in a conventional electric oven). Lightly grease an oven tray.

Combine the flour and sugar in a bowl, and, if desired, the spice. Add the lemon juice and rub in the butter until it resembles fine breadcrumbs.

Lightly beat the eggs and stir in the milk and lemon essence. Add the egg mixture to the dry ingredients and mix with a wooden spoon or fork to form a soft dough, adding a little extra milk if it is too stiff. Add the mixed fruit and stir until well combined.

Drop generous teaspoons of the mixture onto a lightly greased oven tray, allowing room for spreading. Bake for about 15 minutes, or until browned. Loosen the buns and cool on the tray.

MAKES ABOUT 30 BUNS.

Rock Buns

Tips from the cook

- Rock buns should be quite rough on top. To achieve this, make sure the mixture is reasonably stiff and sticky, and don't shape the top after you drop the mixture on the tray.
- Do not sprinkle them with sugar before baking, as suggested in some recipes, if you intend to enter them in competition.

Tips from the judges

- The buns should be even in size (about 5 cm) and colour, with evenly distributed fruit and smooth golden bottoms.
- They should cut well, without crumbling.
- They should be sweet and spicy, with the flavour of the fruit and a delicate hint of lemon.

JAMESTOWN
Banana Cake

Anne Messenger is a relative newcomer to show cooking. Originally from Orroroo, she started out entering sponge classes in the mid 1990s but her enthusiasm has snowballed to the point where she often enters up to 20 classes at a time, and has won the cookery section aggregate at Jamestown on more than one occasion.

Today even her husband Les competes – a diversion from helping to organise the show's cattle section. He has won the men's only chocolate cake competition, and saw one of his cakes auctioned off for a remarkable $30 in the name of charity.

Anne says there are better cooks than her around and she doesn't take it all too seriously, but she likes to support the show by entering as many classes as possible. Promoted as South Australia's best one-day show, the Jamestown event attracts more than 6000 people with a special focus on a different theme every year, as well as agricultural displays, exhibitions and children's entertainment. First held in 1874 and originally known as the Belalie Show, it proved its ongoing popularity with a record gate in 2007.

The following recipe for banana cake has won more than a few blue ribbons. Anne says it comes out light and fluffy like a sponge because of the unusual addition of glycerine, and is 'almost foolproof' to make.

Tips from the judges

- Check the show schedule for specifications about cake size before selecting your cake pan.
- Make sure you follow the class description when it comes to icing. Cake classes are usually quite specific about whether the cake should be iced or not, and sometimes will indicate what flavour of icing should be used.
- Any sign of rack marks or flour on the bottom of your cake will rule it out of contention.

Opposite page, top: Anne and Les Messenger

Opposite page, bottom left: Show ticket – centenary show 1974. First prize card – 1926.

Opposite page, bottom right: Rows of motorcars parked at an agricultural show held at Jamestown, 1923 (SLSA: PRG 280/1/41/55)

Top: Jamestown view

Middle: The Stacey Pavilion, Jamestown showground

Banana Cake

Recipe

125 g margarine (or butter)
3/4 cup sugar
2 eggs
3 bananas, ripened and mashed
1 teaspoon bicarbonate of soda
2 tablespoons milk
1 1/2 cups SR flour
1 teaspoon glycerine

Preheat the oven to moderate (180 °C in a conventional electric oven). Grease and line two log pans.

Beat the margarine and sugar until the sugar is dissolved. Add the eggs one at a time, and beat well. Stir in the bananas.

Dissolve the soda in the milk. Add the milk and flour to the banana mixture, then add the glycerine. Stir until all the ingredients are well combined.

Bake for 20 to 30 minutes, until golden brown and springy to the touch.

Below: Displays of machinery and other items at an agricultural show held at Jamestown, 1923 (SLSA: PRG 280/1/38/296) **Left:** Show book cover, 1962

Tips from the cook

- Farm fresh eggs are critical to success.
- You may substitute butter for the margarine if you prefer.
- One mixture produces two cakes when they are baked in log cake pans.
- Chocolate icing works well with the cake if you are making it for home consumption.
- Glycerine is a sweet, clear liquid used in some icings and fondants. It is available from chemists and supermarkets.

KADINA
Cornflake Biscuits

Gwen Beare and Dulcie Barker took slightly different paths to end up as champion show cooks, but the end results are the same – countless prizes, aggregate trophies and berths as regional finalists in the prestigious State Rich Fruit Cake Championship and State Genoa Cake Competition.

The gregarious Gwen has won both contests and delights in her success at competitive cookery, despite being vision impaired. She only took it up when she was about 60, after a new oven was installed as part of major kitchen renovations. 'That oven has won me a lot of prizes over the years,' Gwen reflects.

Even though she has always loved cooking, and baked every Saturday when her children were small, she soon learnt cooking for shows is quite different. 'You have to be a bit more fussy, my God yes,' she says wryly. 'When I started off show cooking I learnt little by little by looking at other cakes, but I never ever asked for help. I did it all on my own accord.' Perseverance eventually paid off and she beat a serious rival to win the aggregate trophy for cookery across all the Yorke Peninsula shows, having taken home 25 prizes from the same number of entries at one show alone.

These days she only enters a dozen or so classes, with a bit of help from husband Eric who weighs the ingredients because she can no longer read the scales. 'He has to put the mixture in the cake pan too because I would have more out than in, but I do everything else,' she says, pointing out a special raised mark on the oven controls that allows her to set the temperature exactly right.

Unlike Gwen, Dulcie Barker was only 10 when she entered her first show, but her initial focus wasn't cooking: 'I entered a dress in the Moonta Show. It was one I hand-stitched, and I can still remember it; it was a green and white polka-dot sundress.' As an adult she has won aggregates and prizes for everything from cookery to home-killed poultry, and butter made from her own cows' milk. 'I raised my own birds, and did all the killing myself,' she says.

Dulcie is also well known locally for her cake decorating skills. She took it up to earn extra money when her children were young and her husband was involved in a farm accident. Her reputation spread and in 1983 Price's Bakery offered her a part-time job decorating special

Opposite page and above: Dulcie Barker, left, and Gwen Beare

Left: Judges consider entries in a special cake class for local organisations (KAHFSI)

Above: Winner of the inaugural Kadina Show Society Art Prize, 'Show Day' by Heather Cooper (KAHFSI)

Opposite page, left: Cookery section entry form, 1952 (KAHFSI)

Opposite page, right: Kadina show book cover, 1947 (KAHFSI)

occasion cakes for their customers. She is now baking three times a week for a shop in Moonta.

The Kadina Show Society was established in August 1871 and held its first show a month later as a natural progression from early ploughing matches. A three-legged pig and a single-tape fuse made by the Wallaroo Mines Fuse Factory were unusual exhibits at the second show, while South Australian Governor Musgrave added a bit of colour in 1873 when he arrived in a 'handsome wagonette drawn by four spanking grey horses'. The society took up permanent residence at its own grounds in 1882, building a magnificent stone exhibition building which houses the cookery section to this day.

This cornflake biscuit recipe is one of Gwen's favourites. It was given to her a few years ago by a friend. According to Gwen, the challenge lies in cooking them so they are nice and crisp, but still light in colour.

Recipe

Cornflake Biscuits

170 g butter
1 cup sugar
2 eggs
1¾ cups SR flour, sifted
1 cup sultanas
¼ cup chopped walnuts
cornflakes

Preheat the oven to moderately slow (160 °C in a conventional electric oven). Grease an oven tray.

Put the butter and sugar into a mixing bowl. Use a hand-held electric beater or mix-master to beat them steadily for about 5 minutes on a moderate speed, until light and fluffy. Add the eggs and beat a little longer, until well combined.

Using a spoon, stir in the flour, sultanas and walnuts.

Spread some cornflakes out on a flat pan or tray with sides, and crush them slightly with your hand. Take a teaspoon of mix and roll it into a ball. Drop it into the cornflakes and roll until well covered. Place the coated balls onto the pan, 7 cm apart, and press them down very lightly with a damp hand.

Bake for about 20 minutes, or until golden brown.

MAKES ABOUT 80 SMALL BISCUITS.

Tips from the cooks

- Don't make the biscuits too big, particularly if you are making them for competition.
- Don't beat the mixture too hard; set the beater or mix-master to a moderate speed.
- You need to use a large bowl once the butter and sugar are creamed to get an even mixture. Gwen works it by hand at this stage.

Tips from the judges

- The biscuits should be even in colour and size, and snap crisply when they are broken.
- Make sure there are no burnt edges to the cornflakes.

KAPUNDA
Mustard Pickle

The Kapunda Show celebrated its 150th anniversary in 2007, making it one of the oldest agricultural shows in South Australia. The event started as a ploughing match in 1857, only fifteen years after copper ore was discovered in the district, leading to the birth of the state's first commercial copper mining town.

The original ploughing matches expanded by the 1860s to include farm produce and livestock displays, drawing crowds of 3000 to 4000 people. When the mine closed in the 1870s the town continued to develop as the centre for a thriving pastoral industry. While its fortunes have fluctuated over the years, the Kapunda and Light Agricultural Society has always strived to promote agriculture, horticulture and industry in the district.

Today crowds gather in a long shed to view entries in the popular cookery and preserves sections. This is usually where you will find Mavis Lee, who has been convenor for both sections since 2001. An enthusiastic cook, she only started competing in the late 1990s but

has had great success. In 2007 she won eleven out of twelve classes entered in cookery alone and took out the champion preserves ribbon.

Mustard pickle is a long-standing favourite at shows across the state. Here is Mavis's tried-and-true prizewinning version.

Recipe

1 medium cauliflower
2 large onions
salt
750 ml white vinegar
3 tablespoons plain flour

1 tablespoon mustard powder
$1\frac{1}{4}$ cups sugar
$\frac{1}{3}$ cup treacle
2 teaspoons turmeric

Chop the cauliflower and onions into small, even-sized pieces. Combine in a bowl and sprinkle with salt. Cover and let stand overnight.

Place the vinegar in a large saucepan and bring to the boil. Drain and rinse the vegetables and add them to the vinegar. Boil for about 15 minutes, until soft.

Mix the flour, mustard, sugar, treacle and turmeric into a smooth paste and stir into the boiling mixture. Continue to boil for another 3 minutes.

Put into clean, hot jars while still hot, and seal.

Tips from the cook

- Cutting the vegetables into small pieces works better if using the pickle in a sandwich. If you are planning to serve it alongside cold meats, a chunkier style is fine.
- Mavis adds extra mustard for her 'home' version to create a hotter flavour.
- The flavour improves after a few weeks so be patient.

Tips from the judges

- Mustard pickle should have a bright yellow colour and plenty of flavour, without being too hot.
- Cut the pieces evenly. Smaller sizes tend to do better in competition.

Opposite page, top: Mavis Lee (far right) overseeing judging at Kapunda in her role as cookery convenor

Opposite page, bottom left: Mavis Lee's winning preserves

Opposite page, bottom right: Spectators viewing the popular indoor classes at Kapunda

Left: Judging mustard pickles

KEITH
Lemonade Scones

For both experienced and aspiring cooks nothing beats the challenge of making the 'perfect' light, fluffy scone. Apart from technique, which is important, there is considerable debate about ingredients.

Inadvertently, the argument may have been settled at the Keith Kountry Fair and Show. To give their cookery section a boost, the show society decided to raise the bar in 2007 by setting up a special scone challenge with $75 in prize money for the best plain, savoury and fruit scones.

Maureen Wagenknecht not only won first prizes in the two classes she entered but had the judges deliberating over her efforts for some time to choose the overall winner. Her plain and savoury scones were made with the same basic recipe, originally sourced from a local community cookbook, which uses lemonade as a 'rising' agent and the key liquid.

Now retired and living in Bordertown, Maureen has competed for many years but says she never really thought of herself as a scone cook until discovering this recipe. 'I believed I couldn't make scones,' she confesses. A championship winner for her cakes, Maureen started entering shows after taking part in a biscuit competition run by the Country Women's Association at Western Flat. 'I made typical farm biscuits, huge things. Someone gave me a few tips, and from there I kept my ears to the ground... I learnt a bit more every year I entered and that is part of cooking,' she says.

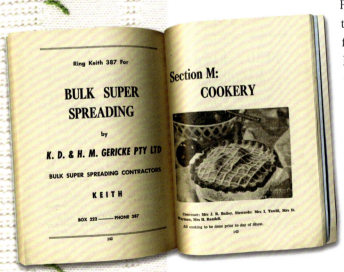

Maureen has been cookery convenor at Keith for about ten years. The indoor sections are well supported, particularly the junior cookery and photography classes, helping to draw a crowd from across the Upper South-East. Keith celebrates its 75th show in 2008.

Recipe

4 cups SR flour
300 ml cream
375 ml lemonade

Preheat the oven to hot (220 °C in a conventional electric oven).

Sift the flour into a large bowl. Add the cream and lemonade and mix lightly with a knife until it forms into a ball.

Turn the dough onto a lightly floured board and pat it out until it is about 2.5 centimetres high. Cut it into rounds and place them on a baking tray, fairly close together.

Bake the scones in a hot oven for about 10 minutes, until golden brown.

MAKES 20 SCONES.

Variation: Savoury scones

Add grated cheese, chopped chives and bacon to taste, and a pinch of cayenne pepper, before adding the cream and lemonade.

Tips from the cook

- Make sure your oven is really hot.
- Don't over-work the mixture – use a knife to stir the ingredients together. Maureen doesn't knead the dough; she just pats it out lightly.
- Don't put too much flour on the board when you are rolling them out.
- Don't twist the cutter when you press it down into the dough and remove it – it will alter the shape when they rise in the oven.
- Use good quality SR flour.

Tips from the judges

- After they are cooked, brush any surface flour off the scones, using a tea towel.
- Cut them out using a proper scone cutter.
- Show scones are round not square – it's one of those unwritten rules. They should be well risen, with smooth, slightly rounded tops and about 5 cm across.

Opposite page, top: Maureen Wagenknecht

Opposite page, bottom: Pages from the 1969 Keith and Tintinara Show Society show book (KTDSSI)

KIMBA
Chocolate Cupcakes

The program for the very first Kimba show in 1921 reflects two worlds; one about to disappear from rural Australian communities and the other emerging in a rush of technological change that would alter farming forever. Lining up in the horse section are classes for the best pair of plough horses and team of four draught horses in a wagon. Towards the back of the program is an advertisement for the new Ford one-ton truck: 'For bringing the City markets nearer . . . Displace your three horses and three men and put more money into the bank.'

The program also lists eleven 'confectionary' classes, offering lucrative first prizes for a collection of homemade sweets, bread, pound and seed cakes, sponges, scones, puddings, tarts, sausage rolls, fancy cakes, cream puffs, Cornish pasties, and jam rolls 'made by girl under fourteen, to weigh not less than 1 lb'.

Many of these classes remain on today's cookery schedule, but you can now try your hand at an infinite variety of sponges – a favourite with Dianne Hamlyn. Showtime usually coincides with one of the busiest seasons on the farm for Dianne, so she prefers baking that doesn't take too long in the oven. 'We shear when the show is on so I usually cook sponge cakes. I know I can do it and they will come out reasonably well and it doesn't take very long,' she says.

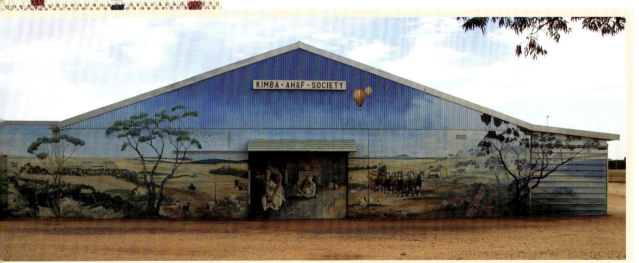

Kimba's cookery convenor, Dianne has been competing since she was a child, one of several show cooks in her family, including her mother Connie Whitwell, who still competes. Dianne thinks this chocolate cupcake recipe may have come from her mother's family. She has been using it for 30 years or so, both in competition and for family occasions. 'I chose it because I have tried a few over the years and they are always dry. These are nice moist cakes,' she says.

Recipe

90 g butter
90 g (1/3 cup) castor sugar
2 eggs
140 g (3/4 cup) SR flour
15 g (2 level tablespoons) cocoa powder
pinch of salt
2 tablespoons milk

Preheat the oven to moderate (180 °C in a conventional electric oven).

Beat the butter and sugar until light and fluffy. Add the eggs one at a time, beating between additions.

Sift together the flour, cocoa and salt and add to the butter mixture in two lots, alternating with the milk.

Spoon the mixture into small patty pans. Bake for about 15 minutes, or until firm.

MAKES ABOUT 20 CUPCAKES.

Opposite page, top: Dianne Hamlyn (KC)
Opposite page, bottom: Community mural at the Kimba showground

Tips from the cook

- The first step in the process is the most important – make sure the butter and sugar are beaten properly, until the sugar is almost completely dissolved.
- Cook each cake in two patty pans to support a better shape.
- Top the cakes with chocolate icing. Or to make butterfly cakes, cut a circular section out of the top (to a depth of about 2 cm) and fill each cake with a small amount of strawberry jam and then cream. Top them with wings made from the circles of cake cut into halves, and dust them with icing sugar.

Tips from the judges

- The cakes should be small and dainty. Try sitting the patty pans in a muffin tray to create a neat and uniform shape.
- The cakes should rise to the top of the patty pans and be nicely rounded. There should be no overhang from overfilling or flattening from too soft a mixture.
- The cakes should have a fine, moist texture with no loose crumbs or holes.
- The cakes must be presented in the patty pans they are cooked in, unless the schedule indicates otherwise, and the cases should peel off easily.

KINGSCOTE
Economical Steamed Plum Pudding

Grace James remembers squeezing into the family buggy as a child and travelling about 30 kilometres on dirt roads to the Kingscote Show:

The buggy was a two-seater, each seat sitting three people, with a small part at the rear where some of us children sat nursing various entries, such as bowls of pansies floating in water and various cooking entries. Our mother [Olive Mabel Elsegood] used to enter in all the sections. She grew beautiful flowers and was an excellent cook, receiving many prizes.

Born and bred on Kangaroo Island, Grace was one of eight children who all went on to compete in the Kingscote Show at some stage. Her father, Frederick Charles Elsegood, was a 'real old battler' who worked hard in a variety of jobs before buying the family farm. In later years, transport arrangements improved and the family travelled to the show in relative comfort on the back of a Chev truck, owned by their neighbour Bob Wheaton. The truck now sits in the Kingscote Museum. 'The show was a great outing for the family,' says Grace, whose most treasured possessions include a photo of the Elsegoods sitting down to a picnic lunch at the showground sometime in the late 1920s.

The Kangaroo Island Agricultural and Horticultural Society's show started in 1911. Today the one-day event attracts about 1500 people, with a strong emphasis on entertainment for young people. Exhibitor numbers are healthy too, with a range of sections reflecting the island's agricultural produce, from wool and grains, to honey and bee products, and commercial wines made from local fruit.

Grace remains an active participant at 85 years of age, and brought home 20 prizes from 28 entries in 2007. She still uses a wood stove to cook, but you won't find any kitchen scales when she is at work. 'I don't use scales for anything. All my cooking is done by a cup and spoonful of this or a pinch of that,' she says.

Grace is particularly well known for her steamed plum pudding. This recipe has won seven first prizes.

Tips from the judges

- Allow a little time for the pudding to set before turning it out to avoid cracks.
- Use a layer or two of foil to help seal the basin, even if you have a basin with a tight-fitting lid.
- The pudding should have a neat even shape, showing it has been cleanly removed from the basin, with no white specks on the surface.

Recipe

2 cups plain flour
1 cup brown sugar
2–2½ cups mixed fruit (currants, raisins, chopped dates)
12 almonds, chopped
1 dessertspoon mixed spice
¼ teaspoon lemon essence
1 large tablespoon butter
2 tablespoons sherry (optional)
2 teaspoons bicarbonate of soda
2 cups boiling water

Grease an 8 cup pudding basin.

Place the flour, sugar, fruit, almonds, spice and lemon essence in a large bowl.

Melt the butter in 1 cup of boiling water and add to the flour mixture. Stir in the sherry, if desired. Dissolve the soda in the remaining cup of boiling water, and add. Mix well.

Spoon the mixture into the greased pudding basin. Cover the basin with greased paper and then foil. Make the cover large enough to fit well over the lip and secure tightly with string.

Place the basin in a large saucepan with enough boiling water to come halfway up the sides of the basin. Cover and boil for about 3 hours.
SERVES 10 TO 12 PEOPLE.

Opposite page: Grace James (GJ)

Below: The Elsegood family at the show, c. late 1920s; Grace is pictured second from left (GJ)

Tips from the cook

- Always use the same sized cup to measure the flour, sugar and water.
- Grace often substitutes 1 cup of commercial mixed fruit, which contains lemon peel, for 1 cup of the listed dried fruits and the lemon essence.
- The batter should be reasonably sloppy. If it's too firm the pudding will not turn out as moist as it should.
- Allow some room in the basin for expansion.
- Make sure you don't let the saucepan boil dry. If the level of water gets too low, add a little more.
- To stop the pudding burning on the bottom try standing the pudding basin on a wire rack (or upside down saucer) placed inside the saucepan.

KINGSTON
Raspberry Jam Roll

The chooks know when showtime is approaching in the Maczkowiack household. Seven days before the Kingston event in early October, they are put on a special diet. 'I like pale egg yolks so a week before the show, we stop feeding them any green feed,' Marjorie explains.

Marjorie has been competing at shows across the Limestone Coast for more than 50 years. Even in her eighties she is in the habit of staying up all night before her local show, preparing entries. She has won a perpetual trophy for cockles nine times but it is her prizewinning jam rolls that have crowds queuing in the street on Easter Saturday at a special fundraising stall.

Marjorie reckons she has made thousands of these velvet-textured wonders for family, friends, community groups and shows. Her recipe isn't written down, but she has the technique down to a fine art.

'I always loved cooking,' Marjorie says. 'I don't know why, I have just always liked it.' One of seven children, she remembers her mother was a good cook too but shooed them out of the kitchen. Instead Marjorie learnt from 'trial and error', working as a cook at a boarding house in Victor Harbor and as a shearers' cook, before settling with her husband Rodney on a farm at Blackford. The couple moved to Kingston in the early 1970s, where they have a small vegetable garden as well as the chooks and a few ducks, supplying dozens of fresh eggs for baking.

Children from the local school occasionally visit to learn cooking and Marjorie is generous in sharing her knowledge with aspiring show cooks to encourage more people to enter. The effort is paying off. First held in 1886, the Kingston Show almost folded in the early 2000s but a dedicated group of volunteers have reversed the trend and are rebuilding the annual two-day event which today draws visitors from as far as Adelaide.

Opposite page: Marjorie Maczkowiack (KAPHSI)

Left and below left: Judging preserves at the Kingston Show, 1964 (KAPHSI)

Below: Show book advertisement for a donut maker

Tips from the cook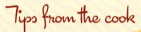

- Drop the pan gently on the benchtop before you put it in the oven – to even the mixture out and remove large air bubbles.
- Apricot jam makes a nice alternative to raspberry for the filling. If you are making it for home try adding whipped cream as well as jam.
- Roll the sponge as soon as it comes out of the oven to avoid cracking. Aim for the filling to create the shape of a curved letter 'C' when you look at the ends.

Recipe

4 eggs
pinch of salt
$1/2$ cup sugar
1 teaspoon vanilla essence
1 cup cornflour

1 level teaspoon bicarbonate
　of soda
1 heaped teaspoon cream of tartar
1 tablespoon boiling water
About $1/4$ cup raspberry jam

Preheat the oven to moderately hot (210 °C in a conventional electric oven). Grease a large, low-sided pan (about 35 cm x 25 cm) and line the base and sides with greaseproof paper. Grease the paper too.

　Separate the eggs. Add the salt to the egg whites and beat with an electric beater at high speed until stiff. Add the sugar and beat until dissolved. Fold in the egg yolks and vanilla. Sift together the cornflour, soda and cream of tartar. Stir gently into the mixture, using a rubber scraper. Add the boiling water and stir in gently.

Tips from the judges

- The filling must be thinly and evenly spread. It should not soak into the sponge.
- Some competitions stipulate that the ends should be cut so check the schedule.
- As an alternative to Marjorie's method, try turning the roll out on to a cloth dipped in hot water and rung out tightly. Remove the cloth immediately.
- You cannot roll a sponge correctly if the ends are crisp or it has dried out because it has been overcooked.
- The completed roll should be plump, not just folded, and there should be no cracks. Some schedules insist that it is rolled only twice, others three times – check the schedule.
- The cake should have the qualities of a sponge, and be of even height throughout. There should be no stickiness caused by undissolved sugar.

Pour the mixture into the prepared pan. Cook for 6 minutes, then gently turn the pan around to ensure an even colour, and cook for another 5 minutes. The sponge is ready when it is golden brown and firm to the touch.

Spread a clean tea towel out on the benchtop or table (make sure it has no creases). Place a piece of greaseproof paper on top of the tea towel and sprinkle it lightly with cornflour.

Turn the roll out immediately onto the paper, and spread thinly with jam. Using the paper and the tea towel, roll it up from the short side, and allow it to cool.

Opposite page: Marjorie and her husband, Rodney

Above: Marjorie and Mrs Wilson at the 1964 Kingston Show (KAPHSI)

LOXTON
Cinnamon Coffee Cake

Raising eight children didn't slow down Joyce Braun or diminish her love of cooking. After 50 years of competing at local shows she is still going strong, but she has worn out three mix-masters along the way. Mind you, they had more than earnt their keep helping feed the family, producing huge quantities of goodies for local fundraising stalls, and making butter from the family's own cow's milk.

Joyce was sixteen when she started competing in the local show, inspired by her mother who was also a show cook (two brothers went on to become commercial bakers). 'I might have missed ten years or so since then with travelling and so on but that would be it. The kids knew not to touch anything so I just kept cooking,' she says.

GOING TO LOXTON SHOW, 1911.

GOING TO LOXTON SHOW, 1936

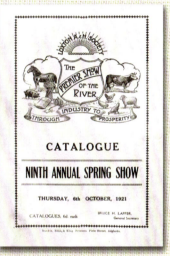

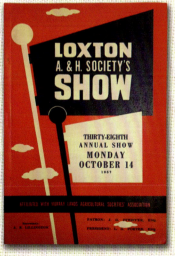

Opposite page, top: Joyce Braun

Opposite page, bottom: Judging preserves at the Loxton Show (LAHSI)

Above: Changing times: illustration from show book comparing modes of transport for showgoers at the first event and 25 years later (LAHSI)

Right from top: Loxton show book covers for 1911 (first show), 1921 and 1957 (LAHSI)

Tips from the judges

- Tea cakes are not high, and the sides should be straight and smooth. The top should be flat or slightly rounded, with no excessive peaking.
- The topping should be carefully and evenly applied, neat and just to the edge of the cake. Some cinnamon is stronger than others so be careful not to over-spice it.

While Joyce gained most satisfaction from making sponges, her cinnamon-topped coffee cake recipe, also known as a tea cake, is a favourite:

I have been using this recipe for a long time. We used to have a deli here for five years . . . and when it came to Thursdays I would bake five big cakes with this recipe, and it would all get sold in the shop. By Thursday night you would hardly have a piece left.

If early records are anything to go by, Joyce is only the latest in a long line of capable cooks in the district. Reports of the first show in 1911 indicate local women 'famous for their cooking' catered for the first official lunch. Although Loxton was a little later than some other Riverland communities in starting up a show, it wasted no time in acquiring grounds and building a hall, ring and livestock yards with donated materials and labour. A little more than four months after a public meeting agreed to the venture, more than 1000 people poured into the new grounds, with seven cars travelling a remarkable distance from Adelaide and paddle-steamers bringing patrons from along the River Murray. Today Loxton hosts a two-day event with extensive competitive classes and entertainment programmes.

Recipe

250 g butter
2 cups sugar
6 drops lemon essence
5 eggs
2½ cups plain flour
1 level teaspoon bicarbonate of soda
2 level teaspoons cream of tartar
1 cup milk
extra butter
extra sugar
cinnamon

Grease a large square pan (about 36 cm), line the bottom with paper, and grease the paper. Preheat the oven to moderate (180 °C in a conventional electric oven).

Cream the butter and sugar until the sugar is dissolved. Beat in the lemon essence and then the eggs one at a time.

Sift together the flour, soda and cream of tartar. Add the dry ingredients to the mixture, with the milk, and beat lightly until smooth.

Place the mixture in the pan and bake for 20 to 30 minutes.

While the cake is still warm, spread generously with extra butter, and sprinkle with sugar and cinnamon.

Tips from the cook

- Use generous amounts of butter, sugar and cinnamon on top.
- Leave the cake in its pan to cool.
- Make sure you beat the butter and sugar properly, until the sugar is dissolved and the mixture is pale, light and fluffy.
- Joyce tends to use just slightly less than a full cup of sugar when she is measuring it – she says too much sugar can cause the cake to drop.

Opposite page: Children and adults waiting to welcome important visitors to the opening of Loxton Show, c. 1914 (SLSA: PRG 280/1/11/51)

Left: Cookery schedule heading, 1918 show book (LAHSI)

LUCINDALE
Fig Jam

Sheila and Keith Bates rely on their extensive garden for most of the fruit and vegetables they use in their prizewinning preserves. The couple bought the block next to their house in Lucindale and planted it out with fruit trees not long after they moved into town in the 1980s.

Originally from Eyre Peninsula, Sheila started competing in shows when she was about fifteen, following in the footsteps of her mother. 'I got first prize for my homemade bread, probably seventy years ago,' Sheila says. 'Mum was always a cook and showed at the Lipson, Yallunda Flat and Cummins shows. Because she did it, I suppose I thought I could too.'

Keith and Sheila moved to the district in the early 1960s to farm almost 1250 hectares allocated from a new subdivision by the lands department. They had been sharefarmers but welcomed the opportunity to set up their own enterprise despite the initial challenges. 'We brought two little boys with us and it was a wet winter and there was just a shed on the block,' Sheila recalls.

The couple have been involved in the local show since they arrived. They both cook for the event – Keith has won the men's chocolate cake competition a couple of times and Shelia has had considerable

success with beer cakes and home-dried apricots. 'We enjoy the competition side of it. It makes a show more interesting if you have got exhibits, and you like to beat someone else,' Sheila admits.

Due to stage its 110th annual show in 2008, the local society has reinvented its main event in recent years to draw larger crowds. Yard dogs, a speed shearing competition, a ute muster which draws entries from interstate, and the Great Southern Muster Concert featuring leading country music performers take centrestage alongside more traditional elements. The society also runs a separate horse show every autumn, but the focus for Sheila and Keith is the spring event where they have scored considerable success with fig jam. Sheila says it's a nice, easy recipe and a traditional favourite.

Recipe

1.8 kg sugar
2.25 kg figs
1 cup water
1 level teaspoon tartaric acid

Place the sugar in a very slow oven to warm.

Wash the figs and remove the stems. Chop the fruit roughly and put it in a large saucepan with the water.

Boil for 10 minutes at a moderate rate, stirring continuously, until the fruit is soft and well cooked. Add the sugar and the tartaric acid, and stir until it returns to the boil. Boil for another 20 to 30 minutes stirring frequently, until the jam is set.

Pour into warm sterilised jars and seal while hot.

Tips from the cooks

- It's important that the figs are clean and in good condition, although they can be quite ripe. You can use either green or black figs.
- Use your hands to 'mulch' the fruit before you cook it to help break it up and bring out the juice.
- Warm sugar dissolves faster and reduces the time it takes to return the jam to the boil.
- To test when the jam is set, place a few small drops on a cold saucer, wait a minute or two, and then push the jam with your finger – it is ready if the jam wrinkles.

Tips from the judges

- Make sure the jars are clean and polished with a soft cloth.
- The accepted standard size of jars for showing is usually about 500 ml but check the schedule.
- The jam should be bright and of a smooth dropping consistency.

Opposite page, top: Shelia and Keith Bates

Opposite page, bottom right: The popular Speed Shears event (PR)

Left: Regan Burow with the champion bull, Yerwal State Bandit (PR)

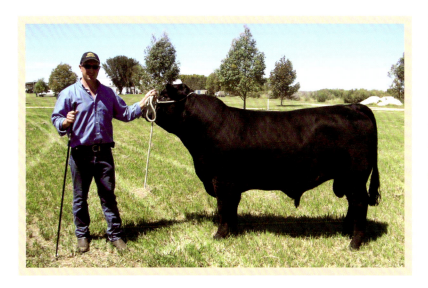

MAITLAND
Maud's Ginger Apricot Crunch

Gwen Smart fondly remembers sitting down with friends and neighbours at local social events and swapping recipes. She tucked them away in a special folder, alongside notes from the legendary Yorke Peninsula cooks who helped Gwen find her feet in the local community and discover the world of show cooking.

Originally from Gladstone, Gwen moved to the peninsula in 1956 with her husband Max. He later took up work as a farmhand at Sandilands where the young couple were given a house with an early-model electric stove, on legs. 'That was our first taste of 230-volt electricity,' Gwen said. 'But it started wearing out and breaking down, and then [the owners] put in a lovely oven for me because they knew I loved cooking.'

A few kilometres down the road lived locally renowned cook May Schulze who took Gwen under her wing:

She gave me a terrific lot of help and really pushed me on. She would encourage us to pop down because she wanted us younger girls competing. I would take a cake down and she would give me pointers. I wrote them into my recipe books.

Gwen went on to win Yorke Peninsula's aggregate trophy for cooking four times. Part of the excitement was meeting up with a group of women she got to know through competition. 'We used to swap recipes and bits and pieces. Lifestyles have changed . . . People don't sit around and talk about recipes as much anymore,' she says. She also regrets that the tradition of afternoon teas where people do their own baking seems to be on the wane too.

Gwen volunteered for 26 years as convenor of the Maitland Show's preserves section, retiring in 2007, a year short of the show's 130th anniversary. The event started in 1878 with competitors in ploughing, livestock, machinery, wheat, farmyard and dairy produce vying for £100 in prize money. Classes for draught horses disappeared in 1946 and by the mid 1980s some $3.5 million worth of agricultural machinery was on display.

While she doesn't do as much cooking herself these days, Gwen has kept all her recipes and notes. Among the collection is this slice, named after her mother Maud because Gwen made it for her 90th birthday.

Tips from the cook

- Use good quality ginger biscuits and don't substitute margarine for the butter.
- For an 'all ginger' flavour, substitute the apricots for 2 tablespoons of finely chopped glacé ginger or stem ginger in syrup.

Tips from the judges

- Each piece in a collection must be uniform in size and shape. They must be sharply cut, with no ragged edges or crumbs.
- This slice should be firm and crunchy in texture.

Recipe

125 g butter
½ cup (125 ml) sweetened condensed milk
1 tablespoon golden syrup
375 g ginger nut biscuits, crushed finely
60 g pecan nuts or walnuts, chopped finely
16 dried apricots, chopped finely

Grease a 24 cm square pan with cooking spray and line with baking paper or alfoil.

Place the butter, condensed milk and golden syrup in a small saucepan and cook over a medium heat, stirring constantly until the mixture is smooth. Bring the mixture to the boil and then reduce the heat and simmer for 3 or 4 minutes, until the mixture thickens slightly.

Place the biscuits, nuts and apricots in a bowl. Pour over the condensed milk mixture and stir until well combined.

Place the mixture into the prepared pan. Refrigerate until set. Cut into squares with a sharp knife.

Opposite page, top: Gwen Smart

Opposite page, bottom left: Maitland show book cover for the 100th show, 1977 (MAHFSI)

Opposite page, bottom right: Showground on show day, c. 1930 (SLSA: B 20398)

Below: The Maitland Show prize list cover, 1976 (MAHFSI)

MANNUM
Pinch of Salt Sponge

By rights Margret Green's sponges should be a disaster. She breaks most of the 'golden' rules usually applied to creating these feather-light, golden mountains but it doesn't seem to matter. The Sponge Queen from Bow Hill wins first prize almost every time. The recipe she uses was given to Margret at her kitchen tea when she married in 1966. Guests wrote recipes into an exercise book, giving the bride a wonderful collection of proven favourites to start married life.

'I couldn't cook a sponge until I got this recipe from a friend,' she recalls with a chuckle. 'It's called a-pinch-of-salt sponge but the funny thing is I never use salt . . . I used to separate the egg whites but I don't do that any more either. Now I put the sugar and eggs in together and I beat it. And I don't measure anything.'

Margret has often thought about why her sponges are so successful and she has come to the conclusion it's more about her trusty mix-master than anything else. In another technique impossible to replicate for cooks with electric ovens, she puts her mixture into a cold oven. She cooks with gas and knows her oven extremely well, timing the cooking period to the precise minute.

Mannum's first show was held in the late 1800s, although details are sketchy as records were lost in the 1956 flood. The show went into recess during World War II and didn't resume until 1958, with the state government taking over the grounds as a construction camp to build the original water pipeline to Adelaide. Some of the buildings constructed for the project are still in use at the site.

Tips from the cook

- Margret doesn't line her cake pans or dust them with cornflour – she just greases them lightly with a cooking spray because she says judges don't like to see traces of cornflour.
- When you have turned the sponges out, put the pans back over the top and leave them so the cakes cool gradually.
- If one half is slightly higher than the other when they come out of the oven, always put the thinner section on the top – it won't squeeze the bottom layer as much and they will end up looking very similar in height.
- If the show catalogue stipulates the sponges must be filled with jam but not which kind, use a light-coloured jam like apricot.

The society continues to play a role in providing information about the latest farming practices – it is very proud of a special commendation received for its efforts to raise awareness about environmental management. Between 2500 and 3000 people attend the event, with entries in the cooking section on the rise.

Recipe

3 medium-sized eggs
½ cup sugar
¾ cup cornflour

1 level teaspoon cream of tartar
½ teaspoon bicarbonate of soda
1 heaped teaspoon plain flour

If you are cooking in an electric oven, preheat the oven to moderately hot (190 °C in a conventional electric oven). Prepare two deep, round 18 cm cake pans by spraying them lightly with oil.

Beat the eggs and the sugar until very pale and fluffy – use a mix-master or hand-held electric beaters and beat on the highest setting for about 10 minutes.

Combine the cornflour, cream of tartar, soda and flour and sift it into the mixture. Remove the beaters and use them to very gently fold in the dry ingredients until combined.

Pour the mixture gently into the prepared pans. If you are cooking with gas, put the tins into a cold oven, in about the middle, and set at 180 °C.

Cook for 20 to 25 minutes, until golden brown. The cakes should be springy to the touch and starting to pull away from the sides of the pan.

Turn the sponges out on to a clean cloth to cool.

Opposite page, top: Margret Green **Opposite page, bottom:** Mannum view

Below right: Margret's trusty mix-master at work

Tips from the judges

- There are many different types of sponges and sponge classes so read the schedule carefully – some specify no cornflour so this recipe will not be suitable.
- Both layers of a sponge must be baked at the same time, using the one mix.
- The top of the sponge should be flat, the texture light and soft, immediately springing back when touched. If the top is sticky you haven't mixed the sugar properly or your oven was too cool.
- If your sponge is flat and tough in texture, it could be because you didn't beat the eggs and sugar enough, you were too enthusiastic in folding in the dry ingredients, or your oven was too cool.
- Sponges 'sink' when you add too much sugar, your oven is too hot, or you remove the sponge before it is cooked properly.

MELROSE
Boiled Fruit Cake

One of nine children, the late Mollie McCallum grew up in a show-minded family and began exhibiting at a very young age. A life member of the Mount Remarkable Agricultural Society, which stages the Melrose Show, Mollie was one of its greatest supporters – a convenor of both flower and needlework sections and a passionate cook whose cakes are fondly remembered across the district.

'Mollie probably learnt to cook because she had to, growing up in such a large family; but she continued to cook because she wanted to. She gained great pleasure from sharing her products with family, friends and visitors,' recalls niece and show secretary Sue McCallum.

Boiled fruit cake was her specialty, not just in competition but as the centrepiece for family occasions. Mollie never married but she cooked for all her brothers and sisters, their spouses, 27 nieces and nephews, 71 great nieces and nephews, and a good many other households in the district. She would often turn up on the doorsteps of people in need with a homemade cake or biscuits.

On show day, her little car would be full of not only her own extensive entries, but exhibits that she had collected from people who were unable to attend through either illness or absence . . . But the truly remarkable thing about Mollie was that she achieved all of these feats with a congenital disability of her left hand – a club hand. She was born in 1922 at a time when there was very little professional help for people with disabilities but grew up to become an independent, competent woman who eagerly attempted any challenge that was presented to her.

Mollie died in 2001 at the age of 79. Although the family is not certain of its origins, her boiled fruit cake recipe is believed to be more than 100 years old, surpassing the age of the Melrose Show itself, which started in 1917. The first event was staged close to a new railway line which allowed patrons to disembark across the road and exhibits to be unloaded from rail trucks directly onto the grounds. Despite many social and technological changes the show remains a popular annual event staged on what is still one of the prettiest showgrounds in South Australia.

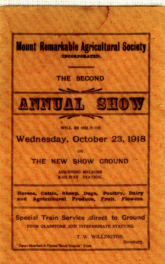

Opposite page: Mollie McCallum (SM)

Above: The luncheon marquee at the 1918 Melrose Show (MRAS)

Far left: An advertisement for the 1918 show luncheon and afternoon tea (MRAS)

Left: 1918 Melrose show book cover (MRAS)

Recipe

750 g sultanas
500 g seeded raisins
500 g currants
250 g mixed peel
125 g cherries
125 g dried apricots, chopped
1 cup water
1 cup rum (or orange juice)
500 g butter (or margarine)
500 g brown sugar
1 tablespoon treacle
1 teaspoon bicarbonate of soda
500 g plain flour
125 g SR flour
$\frac{1}{4}$ teaspoon salt
10 eggs

Place all the fruit in a large saucepan or stockpot. Add the water, rum (or orange juice), butter, and sugar and bring just to the boil, stirring occasionally.

Remove from the heat and stir in the treacle and soda. Cover with a lid and stand overnight.

Next morning, preheat the oven to slow (150 °C in a conventional electric oven). Grease and line a deep 23 cm square cake pan.

Sift together the plain and SR flours and salt. Beat the eggs well and add them alternately to the fruit mixture with the sifted flour.

Spoon into the prepared cake pan and make sure the mixture is evenly distributed. Bake for 3 hours.

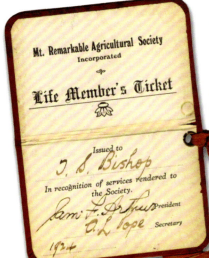

Left: A 1924 life member's ticket for the Mount Remarkable Agricultural Society (MRAS)

Below: Melrose showground, 1932 (MRAS)

Tips from the cook's family

- You can use any combination of dried fruit and almonds, to a weight of 2.25 kg.
- The recipe makes a beautiful, rich Christmas cake.

Tips from the judges

- A well-prepared cake pan is extremely important. Make sure the pan is well greased and lined carefully with several thicknesses of paper, without wrinkles.
- To fill the cake pan, start by spooning in the mixture to a depth of about 2 cm and then work the mixture well down to eliminate air pockets, being careful not to wrinkle the lining. When all the mixture is in the pan, bump it on the bench to settle it.
- The cake should have a smooth appearance on the top, bottom and sides, and should be moist to the touch, with a shiny surface.
- (See State Rich Fruit Cake section for more information.)

MIL LEL
Chocolate Peppermint Slice

Top: Margaret Douglas and her daughter, Helen Swinney

Right: Show patrons inspecting the cookery section on show day at Mil Lel (RH)

A farming district eponymous with a well-known brand of cheese, Mil Lel stages one of the state's smallest annual shows a few kilometres north of Mount Gambier. The event has developed a reputation for the outstanding calibre of its horse section, operating seven separate rings, and attracting more than 1000 entries. The district has also fostered some of the region's best cooks since the first show drew a crowd of about 1000 in 1939. Among today's competitors are Margaret Douglas and her daughter Helen Swinney.

Margaret started competing as a young girl more than 50 years ago. She has been indoor secretary at Mil Lel for more than 20 years and is cooking convenor for the Mount Gambier Show. Helen entered her first show at the age of seven. 'I have always been a show person,' says Margaret, who keeps all her prize cards in an orderly file. 'I find cooking for the show easier than thinking what I am going to cook for myself.'

Mother and daughter have often competed against each other over the years, using the same recipes and working in the same kitchen, which can make life difficult for the judges. 'When you use the same oven and the same tins, things turn out very similar . . . You might have been a bit more heavy handed when you were measuring

or one's a bit browner than the other but that's it,' Helen explains.

Both women have won first prizes for this no-bake chocolate peppermint slice, which is also a family favourite.

Recipe

Base
125 g butter
200 ml sweetened condensed milk
1 (250 g) packet Marie biscuits
1 rounded tablespoon cocoa powder
¼ cup desiccated coconut

Filling
1 cup icing sugar mixture
2 tablespoons butter, melted
1 tablespoon milk
¼ teaspoon peppermint essence

Topping
125 g dark cooking chocolate
30 g copha

To make the base, melt the butter and condensed milk in a saucepan. Crush the biscuits, and mix with the cocoa and coconut. Pour over the butter and milk and mix well. Press the mixture into a slice pan (about 30 cm x 20 cm), lined with baking paper. Place in the fridge and chill well for 1 hour.

To make the filling, mix together the icing sugar, butter, milk and peppermint. Spread evenly over the chilled biscuit mixture and put it back into the fridge to set.

To make the topping, melt together the chocolate and copha. Spread the chocolate evenly over the filling and allow it to set before cutting the slice into squares.

Tips from the cooks

- The trickiest part of the process is applying the chocolate icing. Work quickly to get it smooth before the icing starts to set. Make sure the slice is at room temperature. Spread the topping out with a spatula and then gently shake the pan from side to side so it settles out smoothly.
- Add a bit more butter if the base isn't moist enough. The ingredients need to stick together.
- Use icing sugar mixture not pure icing sugar for the filling. The mix should be very stiff in consistency as it will only set a little. Add more icing sugar if necessary.
- Make sure the slice is at room temperature before you cut it, and put the knife in hot water to make cutting easier without cracking the icing.

Tips from the judges

- Make sure each piece is the same size, and that the sides are perfectly straight and perpendicular. Use a ruler if you have to.
- If it's going to be part of a mixed plate of slices, make sure the other slices are similar in height and scale so they complement each other.
- Don't use pieces from the edge of the pan.

MILLICENT
Nestor's Yeast Buns

An unprepossessing plywood box houses a treasure trove of knowledge that inspires Nestor Buck and her daughter Gloria. Gloria found the box and a house brimming with cooking paraphernalia when her aunt and formidable show cook, Dorothy Alleyn, died in 2001. Infused with the smell of moth balls, it is filled with cookbooks, faded newspaper clippings, and old exercise books containing the favourite recipes of earlier generations, carefully recorded in sprawling blue ink.

Among the collection Gloria spotted a recipe used for the State Rich Fruit Cake Championship and decided she would give it a try. She had never cooked for a show before but regularly drove Dorothy to Adelaide to watch her cakes being judged in state competitions. When Gloria's first cake won a semifinal she cried at the result. 'I couldn't believe it. I never got over it,' she confesses. 'If I hadn't won that competition I don't think I would ever have made another fruit cake.' After that small beginning, this very modest cook went on to win places in the state competition, and then in 2007 she took out the strongly contested Victorian Agricultural Show Senior Rich Fruit Cake title.

While Gloria tends to focus on fruit cakes, Nestor turns her energies to scones, and the 'its and bits'. She only started to make yeast goods when she retired as an industrial nurse, and despite 25 years of experience never gets tired of comparing notes with other breadmakers. She can't remember where she got her recipe for yeast buns, but it has won her many prizes at the three-day Millicent Show, which celebrated 130 years in 2006 and has built an outstanding reputation for its arena entertainment.

Leading riders from four states and bus-loads of enthusiasts from as far as Murray Bridge and Warrnambool are attracted to Millicent on Friday nights to one of the top-ranked motocross events under lights in Australia. A demolition derby also draws a large crowd. Nestor puts her own car to very different use, often parking it in the sun to proof her dough in the back window. She has also been known to cover the tray with a tea towel and put it on an electric blanket, set on high, under a woollen blanket – and says it works a treat.

Nestor's Yeast Buns

Recipe

1 kg bread flour
½ cup sugar
2 tablespoons powdered milk
1 teaspoon salt
1 teaspoon cinnamon or mixed spice (optional)
125 g butter
600 ml water (warm)
2 eggs, beaten
2 tablespoons dry yeast*
2 tablespoons bread improver*
125 g sultanas
125 g currants

Glaze

½ cup milk
2 dessertspoons castor sugar

*the quantity used per kg of flour may vary depending on brand. Check the packet for preferred amounts.

Sift the flour, sugar, milk, salt and cinnamon into a mixing bowl.

Chop the butter, put it in a saucepan with the water and stir until butter melts (there should be no need to put it over heat). Add the two beaten eggs.

Add the yeast and bread improver to the dry ingredients.

Now add the liquid and beat with a mix-master on a slow setting for 5 minutes, using a dough hook, until the mixture is smooth and elastic. Add the sultanas and currants, and beat slowly for another 3 minutes. Make sure all the mixture from the side and the bottom of the bowl is being worked.

Tips from the judges

- Make sure the fruit is evenly distributed through the buns.
- Make smaller versions for competition and keep them well apart during rising and baking, so they don't touch.

Preheat the oven to moderately hot (200 °C in conventional electric oven).

Shape the dough into buns and place them well apart on a lightly greased oven tray. Cover with a clean tea towel and place in a warm spot until they double in size (may take up to an hour).

Bake in the oven for about 10 minutes, until golden brown.

Make a glaze by combining the milk and sugar, and brush the buns with the glaze as soon as they come out of the oven.
MAKES 36 BUNS.

Previous pages, left: Nestor Buck and her daughter, Gloria
Previous pages, right: Nestor Buck making a batch of yeast buns
Opposite page: Judging cakes at the Millicent Show

Tips from the cook

- Make sure the eggs are at room temperature. The water should be warm but not too hot or it will kill the yeast.
- Nestor uses a mix-master fitted with a dough hook to mix her dough. If you are working it by hand, combine the ingredients and knead it for 10 minutes.
- Nestor prefers not to use the spices when she is cooking for shows.

MINLATON
Cumquat Marmalade

The blue-coloured wood stove in the corner of Lil Ramsay's kitchen has been used to prepare food for more than 100 years. She lights it almost every morning, even in summer, and sets a pot of fruit to simmer slowly on its top before going about her daily chores.

> *The stove is part of me really. It was actually my grandmother's... We have it going all day. It heats the hot water for the household and we use it for all the top-of-the-stove cooking. We cook our meat and vegetables, and roast on top of it. It's probably an eyesore to someone else, but it just wouldn't feel right if there wasn't a wood stove in the kitchen.*

Lil and her husband Howard live on the outskirts of Warooka, overlooking the coast and a productive home garden full of fruit trees, berry canes and vegetables. A sign at the front gate encourages visitors to come in and buy jams and pickles, which Lil also sells at a local community shop.

> *My Mum used to make jam and I guess I followed on from there. I don't think there is any great mystery to it. I start all my jams on the wood stove and finish them on the hot plate of the electric stove. I cook the fruit slowly to get it down to a nice thick pulp, and I put the sugar and the jars in the oven, warming and ready to go.*

Lil has only ever been interested in competing at the Southern Yorke Peninsula Show Society's event at Minlaton where she has won countless ribbons for preserves. Entries are displayed in an impressive stone pavilion built in 1881, just three years after the show started. About 3000 patrons attend the annual event which continues to reflect the district's diverse agriculture sector.

Left from top: Minlaton show book covers from 1926, 1954 and 1961 (SYPASI)
Opposite page, top left and right: Historic buildings at the Minlaton showground
Opposite page, bottom: Lil Ramsay bottling jam in her kitchen at Warooka

Tips from the cook

- It's easier to make smaller lots of marmalade than one large amount, although you can double this recipe without affecting the quality.
- Slicing the fruit finely makes it easy to find the seeds.
- It is important that the fruit is soft before you add the sugar.
- Warm the sugar gently in a very slow oven so it doesn't drop the temperature of the fruit when it's added, and it dissolves more quickly.
- Once you have added the sugar, don't let the jam re-boil until the sugar is completely dissolved.
- When it is boiling fast, the marmalade may splatter so make sure your arms are protected. Lil puts sheets of newspaper around the stove and on the floor to make cleaning up easier.
- To find out whether the jam is set, place a few drops onto a cold saucer. Let it cool for a few moments and then push it gently with your finger. If wrinkles form, the jam is ready. Lil tends to put four separate blobs of jam onto the saucer so she can test it several times to make sure.
- Wash the jars and heat them on a tray in the oven. Use cotton garden gloves to handle the hot jars when you are filling them with marmalade.

Recipe

1 kg cumquats, sliced finely and seeds removed

600 ml water

2.5 kg sugar

Put the cumquats and water in a large saucepan and cook slowly, with the lid on, stirring occasionally, until you have a thick pulp and the fruit is soft.

Remove the pan from the heat, and stir in the sugar until it is completely dissolved. Return the pan to the heat. Boil rapidly, with the lid removed, stirring constantly until setting point is reached (about 15 minutes).

Skim any froth off the top with a big spoon. Using a cup, pour the marmalade into warm sterilised jars, filling them to the brim, and put the lids on.

Cumquat Marmalade

Tips from the judges

- If the schedule doesn't state any requirements, present the marmalade in a 500 ml jar with cellophane or screw tops.
- Make sure they are clean and shiny, and that the label is centred properly.
- The marmalade should be fresh, bright, and have a good jelly consistency. There should be no seeds or signs of fermentation or crystallisation.
- The rind should be tender and evenly distributed, and the flavour sharp but not bitter or sugary.

Left: Patrons enjoy a picnic at an early Minlaton Show (MNTM)

MOUNT BARKER
Sue's Sausage Rolls

Sue O'Higgins describes herself as a practical person who likes to create – and she finds cooking the perfect combination. She can remember going to the nearby Uraidla Show as a little girl and searching eagerly for her mother's name on prize tickets in the cookery section. 'She is a brilliant cook,' Sue says. 'In those days there were lots of fancy cakes that we don't have now, and she would enter all of them . . . She got a lot of satisfaction from it; it was very good for her self-esteem.'

One of the earliest show society's in the colony, the Mount Barker Agricultural Association was founded in 1846. The organisation held its first show a year later, and the event rotated between Nairne, Mount Barker and Woodside until 1878 when it took up permanent residence at the present showground. Now a two-day highlight of the growing town's autumn calendar, the event went into recess for 26 years before being revived by an energetic committee in 1989.

A year later Sue entered it for the first time and has competed ever since. 'It became a real family affair with my daughters, my husband and myself entering, sometimes successfully, sometimes not. But life changes and now it's only myself who is still involved,' says Sue, who has served as a convenor, steward and assistant show secretary.

Sue's sausage rolls nearly always gain a prize when she enters them, and they are popular at social events too. The recipe is her mother's, adapted to use commercial sausage meat and good-quality commercial puff pastry. The end result is a quick snack more suited to busy lifestyles than the traditional version.

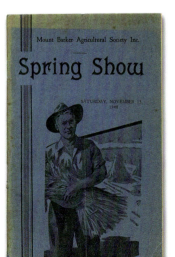

Above: Sue O'Higgins

Left: Show book covers from the autumn and spring shows at Mount Barker, 1948 (MBASI)

Above: A large display of produce at an agricultural show at Mount Barker, 1920 (SLSA: PRG 280/1/22/132)

Below: Display of prizewinning vegetables at the Mount Barker Show by Messrs Halliday Brothers, c. 1930 (SLSA: SRG 168/1/58/4)

Recipe

7 slices fresh bread
1 small onion (optional)
¼ cup parsley, finely chopped
500 g sausage mince
2 sheets commercial puff pastry
1 egg, beaten

Preheat the oven to moderately hot (200 °C in a conventional electric oven). Grease an oven tray or line with baking paper.

Crumb the bread in a blender. If you are intending to use the onion, process it at the same time. Put the bread, onion, parsley and sausage mince in a large bowl and use your hands to make sure the ingredients are well combined. Divide the mixture into four equal portions.

Cut each pastry sheet in half. Lay one portion of the mixture on each piece of pastry, shaping it into a long sausage down the centre of the pastry. Roll the pastry tightly around the mince. Using a sharp knife, trim the ends and cut each roll into five equal pieces, about 5 or 6 centimetres long. Mark the top with a fork or knife. Glaze with the beaten egg.

Cook for 20 mins, or until golden brown.

MAKES 20 SAUSAGE ROLLS.

Opposite page: Sue O'Higgins making sausage rolls

Tips from the cook

- Using onion will make the sausage rolls softer.
- When you have made the filling, it should be a little sticky but not 'gluey'. Your fingers should come away from the mixture easily. If it's too sticky add more bread.
- Try to keep the pastry cool so it's easier to handle.
- Cut one sausage roll and use it as a template. The sausage rolls will shrink in length as they cook – you should get five out of each half-sheet of pastry.

Tips from the judges

- Most shows ask for a selection of six sausage rolls. Make sure the sausage rolls are all the same length, even in colour on all sides, and cut square and perpendicular at each end.

MOUNT GAMBIER
Ginger Fluff

Beryl Hill has made more ginger fluffs than she can count, but she still checks the recipe every time. The first woman to serve as president of Mount Gambier's show society, she has been competing in the Lower South-East for more than 50 years. These days her entries line up alongside those of her daughter, Judith Wood, another formidable show cook, and Judith's son, Geoffrey, who is fiercely competitive and has been known to beat them both.

Beryl started show cooking in 1956 and is best known for her ginger fluff – an exquisitely light, spice-tinged sponge based on a recipe she found many years ago in a Country Women's Association calendar. She uses her own fresh eggs and a wood stove, but she says there is really no great mystery to successful baking. 'Just follow the recipe, that's the most important thing, and if you are showing read the schedule. So many times people don't do that.'

Despite vowing to retire, Beryl can't resist filling in the entry forms when the next season comes around. 'I quite enjoy it. It's taken me away from home and I really like being involved,' she admits. The rest of the family seems to agree. Judith has been competing since she was at primary school and Geoffrey is a veteran at 17.

What does he like about show cooking? 'Winning,' he answers very directly. 'Trying to get it right – the challenge,' he adds. Ginger fluff is his favourite too, although he uses a slightly different recipe to his grandmother, and takes care to sift the flour three times instead of only twice. There must be something in it because Geoffrey won champion cake in the open section of the Mount Gambier Show in 2007.

The event attracts about 10,000 people over three days. Like many other country shows its forerunner was a ploughing match, to foster skills in a burgeoning agricultural community. The first show in 1861 was spoilt somewhat by rain, an ongoing challenge for organisers who have learnt to cope with the region's unpredictable spring weather in planning regular new features to complement trade exhibits, livestock classes, horses in action, and an extensive sideshow alley.

Top: Volunteers prepare food for the show luncheon at the Mount Gambier Show, 1959 (TBW)

Middle: Students during a cooking class in Mount Gambier, 1958 (SLSA: BRG 347/1523)

Bottom: Cookery judge Mrs H.E. Holzgrefe and steward Mr L.B.J. Uphill prepare to judge cookery entries, 1958 (TBW)

Top: Beryl Hill, her daughter Judith Wood and grandson Geoffrey (YJ)
Above: Mount Gambier showground grandstand crowd, early 1900s (HF)

Tips from the cooks

- Beryl prefers her eggs to be no more than three days old because she says older eggs do not whip up the same.
- If you use castor sugar, use slightly less than the amount (of sugar) given in the recipe.
- To make sure the two halves of your cake are even, weigh the cake pans once they are lined, and then re-weigh them after you have poured in the batter.
- Fill the cake with cream and dust it with icing sugar to serve at home.

Top left: Johanna Aldersey looking after piglets in the Elders Agricultural Learning Centre at the 2007 Mount Gambier Show (TBW)

Top right: Competitors in the novice underhand woodchopping championships (TBW)

Above: Cooper Ferguson enjoys riding a toy tractor (TBW)

Right: Adam Munro's dog Missy competing in the yard dog trials (TBW)

Recipe

4 eggs, separated
pinch of salt
$^3/_4$ cup sugar
$^1/_2$ cup cornflour
2 dessertspoons plain flour
2 level teaspoons ground ginger
2 level teaspoons cinnamon
1 teaspoon cocoa powder
1 teaspoon cream of tartar
$^1/_2$ teaspoon bicarbonate of soda
1 dessertspoon golden syrup

Use cooking spray to grease two 20 cm round sandwich pans and line the base with greaseproof paper. Preheat the oven to moderate (180 °C in a conventional electric oven).

Put the egg whites and the salt in a very large bowl and beat with a hand-held electric beater or mix-master on high speed until stiff peaks form (about 10 to 15 minutes). If you are using a mix-master, attach the 'whisk' beater.

Continue beating on a high speed, and add the egg yolks one at a time, beating until well blended. Add the sugar and beat until dissolved – the mixture should be creamy but reasonably thick.

Sift twice together the cornflour, flour, ginger, cinnamon, cocoa, cream of tartar and soda. Gently fold them into the egg mixture until combined, working quickly but gently.

Add the golden syrup by gently drizzling it from the end of the spoon, scattering it over the top of the mixture. Gently fold the syrup into the batter.

Divide the mixture evenly between the two prepared sandwich pans and bake in a moderate oven for 15 to 20 minutes. The cake is cooked when you touch the top and it springs back. Do not overcook.

Place a thick layer of paper onto a cake cooler rack. Tip the cakes out onto the paper and immediately tip them back onto their bottoms so the tops of the cakes are not spoiled.

Tips from the judges

- The cake should be well risen, very light and fluffy, with a close and even texture. It should have a rich ginger flavour with a slight hint of cinnamon.
- The cake must have two even layers, identical in thickness and baking. Both layers must be baked at the same time using the one mix.
- The top should be flat, and there should be no blisters, sugar spots or stickiness.
- Specifications for filling and decorating a ginger fluff vary between shows so check the cooking schedule.

MOUNT PLEASANT
Mary's Farm Pasties

Mary Starkey is an instinctive cook who genuinely loves baking, drawing on generations of knowledge passed down through the women in her family. But her early efforts in the kitchen were not always successful:

> When I was real little, about nine or ten, we were on a market garden at Lenswood and my mum would go out into the garden and I would be inside making a cake. I would think what could be in it and I would make up the recipe. We had to eat lots of custard and pudding [made from failed attempts] but Mum never put me off.

Mary can remember going to shows with her grandmother, looking at the cookery and thinking 'maybe one day that would be nice to do'. She was already exhibiting when she met her husband, Lyall, whose family has been involved in the Mount Pleasant Show for more than 100 years with prizewinning Polwarth sheep and wool. She is a regular prizewinner at Uraidla, Mannum and Mount Barker, and has won the aggregate cookery trophy for the region five or six times.

Mary often enters almost every class on the cookery schedule at Mount Pleasant which has more than 50 open classes alone.

> I feel that if I don't put in as much as I can possibly cook then it will be a dying art. What I am trying to do is to encourage the younger generation to put things in to keep the show going. I think that's the biggest thing to me when it really boils down to the nitty gritty.

Her daughter, Kayla, is competing too and is well on the way to replicating the success of her mother, having taken out the regional junior cookery aggregate trophy twice by the age of 11.

Recognised today as one of the best one-day shows in the state, the first Mount Pleasant Show was held in March 1863 on a 'crisp' autumn day which apparently drew such a large crowd organisers had to cut down fences to clear more space around the temporary pavilion. According to local history book, *The Quiet Waters By*, judges

heaped praise on the quality of wheat and barley displayed but were far less flattering about the single wine exhibit: 'To speak the truth we must say that the only entry was most abominable trash, horribly bad and not in any way worthy of a place; we really believe that the exhibitor must have brought it away from home in mistake.' The same would never be said of Mary's old-fashioned, farm-style pasties, a family favourite which have won first prize at the Royal Adelaide Show on more than one occasion.

Recipe

Pastry
4 cups plain flour, sifted
250 g butter (or margarine), chopped
pinch of salt
juice of half a lemon or 2 tablespoons white vinegar
cold water
1 egg

Filling
5 or 6 large potatoes
1 large onion
2 or 3 large carrots
1 medium swede
2 medium turnips
1 cup grated sweet potato
250 g mince beef or lamb
salt and pepper

To make the pastry, place the flour, butter and salt in a large bowl. Rub in the butter until the mixture resembles fine breadcrumbs. Create a well in the centre and add the lemon juice or vinegar and enough water to make a soft dough (start with about half a cup and gradually adding more if necessary). Use a knife to mix the dough.

Tips from the cook

- Leave the meat out and make a filling just using vegetables.
- Make sure the dough is soft but not sticky.
- Mary processes the vegetables with an old cast-iron mincer clamped to her kitchen table when she is baking them for home, but she says it's better to chop them finely for competition so the judges can clearly see the vegetables you have used. If you use a blender, be careful the vegetables do not turn to mush.
- Don't fuss with the pastry – you can usually roll it out straight after mixing without resting it in the fridge. Mary says the lemon juice or vinegar helps create a lighter pastry.
- Use a generous amount of ground black pepper to give the flavour an extra kick.

Opposite page, top: Mary Starkey and her daughter, Kayla.

Opposite page, bottom: Livestock on parade at Mount Pleasant (MPAHFSI)

Tips from the judges

- The pasties should have a uniform size, shape and frill, and a smooth bottom.
- There should be no sign of excess fat, or of filling escaping from the seal or the sides.
- They should be golden brown all over, with no scorched patches on the frill.

Below: Feature decorations on the Mount Pleasant Show Hall

Right: An early show book cover (SRM)

To make the filling, grate or finely chop the potatoes, onion, carrots, swede and turnips. Place them in a large bowl with the sweet potato and meat. Add salt and pepper to taste and mix until well combined, using your hands.

Preheat the oven to moderately hot (190 to 200 °C in a conventional electric oven). Grease a baking tray, or cover it with baking paper.

Create an egg wash by beating together the egg and about 2 tablespoons of water.

Roll the pastry out to 2.5 mm thick and cut into rounds, using a saucer and a sharp knife. Brush the edges of each round with the egg wash and place a large spoonful of filling in the centre of the pastry. Lift opposite sides of the pastry up and pinch them together over the filling to create a frill over the top.

Brush the pasty with egg wash and place on the prepared oven tray. Bake for 30 to 40 minutes until golden brown.

MAKES 10 TO 12 PASTIES.

Above: Marquees and spectators at an event on the showgrounds at Mount Pleasant, 1910 (SLSA: PRG 280/1/3/262)

Below: In between classes in the dairy section (MPAHFSI)

MUNDULLA
Sultana Cake

The South-East township of Mundulla might be small, but its show is a major success story. Known today as the Moot Yang Gunya Festival, the event is held under the shade of majestic gums at one of the state's prettiest showgrounds and features the largest prime lamb competition in Australia.

In her own quiet way, Kathleen Herrmann has also put Mundulla on the map. A regular champion locally for her sultana cakes, Kath found herself in the news for a daring long-distance feat, aided by an interstate bus service. In 2006 Kath decided to put one of her cakes on a McCafferty's bus and send it to the Royal Darwin Show. Her son John, an officer with the Royal Australian Air Force in the Northern Territory, had thoughtfully posted her a cookery schedule. The cake won third prize, so Kath repeated the exercise a year later and came second.

Friends heard about her efforts and, one night over tea at the local bowling club, they urged her to take on the Royal Adelaide Show. 'When the time came I nearly didn't do it,' she says. 'And then I left Mundulla in good time [to drive the cake to Adelaide] and a semitrailer took the lights out at the toll gate.' Despite the traffic chaos, Kath made it to the showground just before the official closing time for delivering entries. Next day she went back as soon as the gates opened to check the results. Much to her astonishment she had won.

Kath has often been told that a sultana cake is one of the most difficult cakes to make well; it is certainly one of the most hotly contested classes in many shows. 'I still say it's the oven that's the secret – to get it even in colour, and no cracks,' she says.

Originally from Naracoorte, Kath learnt to make sultana cake from her mother, Rita Beaton, who was also a champion cook. 'It was the first cake I ever made by myself. I was only about ten or eleven,' she recalls. 'Mum was sick and in hospital for a week . . . and I was home from school and helping. I can still see myself with the book open at the table, making this cake . . . It looked fantastic but it was very salty.'

Adapted from a Country Women's Association cake calendar, Kath says her prizewinning recipe is very similar to her mother's version. Kath started competing at shows in the 1960s after coming third in a major state sultana cake competition organised by the

CWA. She was elected the first woman president of the Mundulla Agricultural Horticultural and Floricultural Society in 1990. Their event has expanded beyond recognition since then. First held in 1898, the show now runs over three days and, unusually, is spread across a range of venues. The prime lamb competition, a two-day 'Stockman's Challenge', showjumping, strong livestock classes, horse events under lights, and Saturday night entertainment draw about 2000 people.

Recipe

375 g butter
375 g sugar
4 eggs
1 teaspoon lemon essence

440 g plain flour
220 g SR flour
375 g sultanas
300 ml milk

Preheat the over to moderate (180 °C in a conventional electric oven).

Line a deep 20 cm square cake pan (if you are using greaseproof paper instead of baking paper, grease the pan and the paper).

Cream the butter and sugar until light and fluffy. Add the eggs one at a time, beating well between each addition. Add the lemon essence.

Sift the plain and SR flours together and fold into the mixture, adding the sultanas and milk alternatively in several lots.

Pour the batter into the prepared cake pan and make sure it is distributed evenly. Bake for $1^{1}/_{2}$ to $1^{3}/_{4}$ hours. Leave the cake in the pan to cool.

Tips from the cook

- Drop the cake pan on the bench before you put it in the oven. It helps remove the air bubbles and evenly distributes the batter.
- Some show cooks and judges do not like the 'shiny' look they say baking paper can give a cake when used to line pans, compared with greaseproof or brown paper, but Kath uses it. She doesn't grease her pan. She uses two pieces of paper placed so they cross over in the bottom of the pan, lining the bottom twice and the sides once. To make sure the pieces meet in the corners without creases, she measures the paper first by lying one edge of the pan along the long side of the paper. She then draws a pencil along the opposite side and cuts the paper to fit, allowing plenty of height up the side of the pan.

Tips from the judges

- The fruit must be evenly distributed.
- The cake should be an even golden colour, and cooked right through.
- There should be no cracks in the top, and no cake rack marks on the bottom.

Opposite page, top: Kathleen Herrmann (KH)

MURRAY BRIDGE
Dried Apricot Jam

When the *Proud Mary* riverboat pulls into the banks of the River Murray at Mypolonga, in-the-know passengers head straight to a small shop operated by the local school. On its shelves are Wendy Uren's jams and marmalades, made from fruit grown in the family's commercial orchard just outside the town.

Wendy has won many prizes for her preserves over the years, but she treasures just as much the feedback from people like a Queensland tourist who wrote to order more because he reckoned her dried apricot jam was the best he'd ever tasted. The apricots she uses are winners in their own right – proving the importance of quality ingredients – as they took out the championship for dried fruit, vegetables and herbs at the 2007 Murray Bridge Show.

Despite water challenges, the Urens are trying to keep a few apricot trees going to supply local markets. Among them are the Moorpark and Hunter varieties Wendy prefers for her jam. In recent years she has also discovered the joy of making bread using a bread-making machine and tends to focus on yeast classes in the cookery section at Murray Bridge.

The town's first show was held in 1909. The society missed a few years because of war and the 1956 floods, and the show has changed location three times, moving to the current grounds in 1966 after a formidable effort by volunteers to build new facilities in less than twelve months. But today's two-day event is a major drawcard, featuring an extensive entertainment program and competitive classes in everything from the usual livestock sections to sheaf tossing and sheep shearing, pets and home brew, whip cracking and donkeys.

Tips from the cook

- Wendy says the drying techniques used by overseas producers have an effect on the quality of the jam, so use Australian apricots.
- Apricot jam sticks to the bottom of the pan easily – stir it at least every 10 minutes or so.
- If you boil the jam too slowly or for too long it will go dark.
- Don't double the recipe – it will affect the quality of the jam. You are better off making smaller lots.
- To test whether the jam is ready, take a small spoonful and put it on a saucer and refrigerate for a few minutes. If the jam is cooked, it will wrinkle up when you push it gently with your finger.

Recipe

1 kg Australian dried apricots
4.5 litres boiling water
3 kg sugar
juice of 1 lemon

Wash the apricots and cut it into small pieces if preferred. Put it in a large pan and cover with the water. Let it stand overnight, or for about 8 hours.

Simmer gently for about 1 hour. Add the sugar and lemon juice, stirring continuously until the sugar dissolves.

Boil rapidly until the jam sets, stirring frequently. Pour the jam into sterilised jars and seal while hot.

For Preserving Time—a **VAPEX PRESERVING OUTFIT,** standard an delectric from only **£7-19-6**

Tips from the judges

- The jam should be bright in colour.
- Make sure your jars are clean and sparkling.

Opposite page, top: Wendy Uren

Opposite page, bottom: Murray Bridge show book covers from 1947, 1949 and 1959 (MBAHSI)

Left: Show book advertisement for Vapex preservers

ORROROO
Macadamia and Wattle Seed Biscuits

When adventurer, entrepreneur and champion of all things Australian Dick Smith agreed to open the tiny Orroroo Show in 2005, local cook Denise Ogilvy decided the occasion merited something special – so she created a biscuit recipe using native bush ingredients. The recipe was published in the show book and people were encouraged to make it for a separate competitive class, with the winner receiving a special trophy.

'We wanted to get some innovation into the cookery section and maybe have something using Australian ingredients,' Denise says. 'I had cooked with wattle seed before. It brings out the nutty flavour in the macadamias. I looked at different recipes but I wanted to have something easy for people to follow, with not too much messing about.'

Formerly vice-president of the Orroroo Agricultural Show Society, Denise has had plenty of experience as a cook, catering for the birthday parties and weddings of her six daughters, and working as a shearers' cook. To make sure the biscuit recipe was a winner, she decided to try them out on her toughest audience. 'I was cooking for shearers when I was putting it together and I practiced on them with it. It has to be good if you can get it past a shearer,' she says.

Orroroo held its first show in 1882 – the same year the town's flour mill won a championship against world competition at the Sydney Exhibition. The local event may have been a more modest affair but it was a 'red letter day' for the community, with special excursion trains bringing patrons to view a grand display of livestock and farm implements. Agricultural and dairy produce, saddlery and poultry were also on display at the Institute Hall, which was decorated with flags for the occasion. By 1891 the event was being described in *The Register* as 'the largest held in the colony', showcasing excellent produce. Orroroo celebrated its 100th show in 2006.

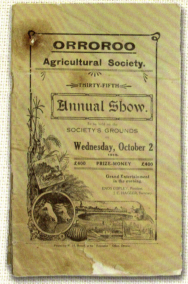

Opposite page: Denise Ogilvy (DO)

Top, left: Orroroo Show Society president Kerry Manning welcomes Australian entrepreneur Dick Smith to the 2005 show; the biscuit recipe was created in his honour (TF)

Top, right: Show book cover, 1918 (OHS)

Bottom, left: Formal letter of invitation to a show judge, 1917 (OHS)

Bottom, right: Orroroo Show lady's membership ticket, 1915 (OHS)

Above: Show book advertisement for an Orroroo baker, 1918 (OHS)

Recipe

250 g butter
1¾ cups castor sugar
2 eggs

plain flour (about 3 cups)
½ cup chopped macadamias
1 tablespoon wattle seed

Preheat the oven to moderate (180 °C in a conventional electric oven). Grease an oven tray.

Cream the butter and sugar until light and fluffy. Beat in the eggs one at a time. Mix in enough flour to form a stiff dough. Knead in the nuts and wattle seed.

Form the dough into balls about the size of a walnut. Place them on a greased tray and press down with a fork. Bake for about 12 minutes, or until golden. Cool on the tray.

MAKES ABOUT 80 BISCUITS.

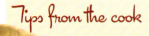

Tips from the cook

- You can keep the uncooked dough in the freezer.
- The amount of flour given is a guide only – you may need more if you use larger eggs or the butter is very soft.

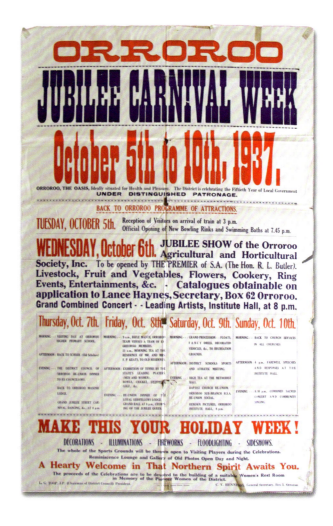

Tips from the judges
- The biscuits should be crisp and evenly cooked.
- If a collection is entered, the biscuits should be similar in size and colour.

Opposite page, left: A show book advertisement for special trains to the Ororoo Show, 1918 (OHS)
Opposite page, right: Poster for the show and the Jubilee Carnival Week, 1937 (OHS)
Above: Show book advertisement for Orroroo Hotel, 1918 (OHS)

PARNDANA
Genoa Cake

Kangaroo Island's Vida Symons was something of a legend in South Australian show cooking circles. At the age of 93 she made it into the final of the 2007 State Genoa Cake Competition. It wasn't the first time; in the first 22 years of the contest Vida, her daughter Claire Stoyel and Claire's daughter Mary-Ann won eleven times, often competing against each other.

This is no mean family feat given the genoa cake is regarded as the 'prima donna' of show cakes – demanding, delicate and potentially the hardest to get right even though winning is not considered quite as prestigious as in the State Rich Fruit Cake Championship, which Vida and Claire have also won.

Vida moved to Parndana with her young family in 1953 as part of a soldier settlement scheme that created the town and about 180 new farms. Claire remembers her mum always cooking for shows, first for Kingscote and then for the Parndana event.

But the challenge that was undoubtedly the focus of her energies was the genoa cake competition. Cooks battle it out at eleven regional semifinals to win a spot in the finals, judged at the Royal Adelaide Show. Vida won the contest for the first time in 1993, while Claire, living in Mount Barker, took out the main trophy in 1991. Vida went on to win the contest four times, as did Claire, while the young and talented Mary-Ann won it three times in succession from 2004.

Top: Vida Symons preparing her entry for the 2007 State Genoa Cake Competition (TI)

Above: Claire Stoyel and her daughter, Mary-Ann

What is it about the contest that so enthralled these women? Claire is not sure, but she thinks it has something to do with the fact that while the recipe looks deceptively simple, it is extremely difficult to make perfectly:

> There is the recipe and then there is the knowledge about how to do it . . . You have to fiddle a long time, experimenting with your oven and cooking times. Your oven plays a fairly big part in it, but it depends on the ingredients and how you mix it too.

Mary-Ann was still in school when she made her first state final. She urges more young people to have a go at competing and help preserve the traditions of show cooking and agricultural shows. 'It's a tradition and it's exciting and a show wouldn't be the same without it,' she says.

Before she died in January 2008, Vida was honorary patron of the Parndana event, started by the soldier settlers in 1957 to exhibit their produce and celebrate the new community. The show maintains a rural focus, including a separate section for honey and bee products, and a long-standing sheep shearing competition.

Recipe

250 g butter
250 g castor sugar
lemon essence (a few drops)
6 eggs (410 g)
400 g plain flour
1 teaspoon baking powder
170 g currants
170 g sultanas
60 g lemon peel
60 g dried figs, chopped
70 g glace cherries
3 tablespoons milk
60 g almonds, blanched and chopped

Preheat the oven to slow (150 °C in a conventional electric oven).

Grease and line the bottom and sides of a deep 20 cm square cake pan, making sure there are no creases in the paper.

Cream the butter and sugar until light and fluffy and the sugar is dissolved. Beat in the lemon essence. Add the eggs one at a time, beating thoroughly in between.

Sift together the flour and baking powder three times. In a separate bowl, combine the currants, sultanas, lemon peel, figs and cherries.

Stir the flour and fruit into the butter mixture in four lots, alternating with the milk until combined. Lastly, fold in the almonds.

Bake for 2½–3 hours, or until golden brown and firm to the touch.

Tips from the cooks

- Be very precise about weighing the ingredients for this cake and make sure you use good quality fruit, flour and sugar. Check the fruit for stalks and remove them.
- Sift the dry ingredients three times.
- Use fresh eggs and have the eggs and butter at room temperature before you start.
- Lining the cake pan properly and to suit your oven is a crucial factor. Vida used brown paper, ironed to make sure there were no creases. Some cooks put extra layers of newspaper around the outside of the pan to stop the sides from browning too fast.
- The genoa cake can be decorated with almonds but Vida preferred not to as it can cause cracks in the top and damage the texture when the cake is cut.

Tips from the judges

- The cake should be baked in a pan with square corners and straight sides.
- The cake is judged on the same criteria as a rich fruit cake (see the Rich Fruit Cake section). It should be a golden brown colour.

PENOLA
Anzac Biscuits

Wartime experiences and decades in age may separate them, but there is no doubt the Anzac biscuit class at the Penola Show represents a meeting of minds and tastebuds. In an innovative approach appreciated by both the competitors and the judges, the show asks representatives from the local RSL branch to choose the best biscuits baked by school students, with the winner receiving $50 to boost their pocket money.

Of course, there were a few rules the enthusiastic diggers had to learn the first time round. Apparently they enjoyed the experience so much they ate all the winner's biscuits. When the stewards returned to check on progress, there was nothing but a few crumbs to put on show.

The oversight didn't seem to worry young Caitlin Fulton who won three champion exhibit ribbons by the age of 13. This eager young cook only started her show career in 2005, and loves making chocolate cake and muffins best, using her mum's cookbooks.

Strongly influenced by early Scottish settlers, Penola also has special cookery classes for shortbread and Dundee cake. The concept would no doubt have pleased Scottish-born pastoralist and Coonawarra Fruit Colony founder John Riddoch who chaired the public meeting that voted to hold the first show in 1864. Only six weeks later exhibitors and patrons gathered in 'perfect weather' at Market Square. The society moved to the current grounds in 1950, and the show continues to go from strength to strength. An innovative highlight drawing attention from beyond the region is a $1000 Grand Champion Rose prize.

Above: Caitlin Fulton

Left: Advertisement from a show book (JH)

Opposite page, bottom: Young show cooks Caitlin Fulton and Bella Minge with Anzac biscuit judges, retired baker and World War II digger, Eric Brand, Peter Ryan and Pat Wilson from the Coonawarra Penola sub branch of the RSL

Tips from the judges

- The collection of biscuits should be uniform in size and shape.
- An Anzac biscuit should break sharply when you snap it. It must be crisp, quite thin and have a nice golden colour.

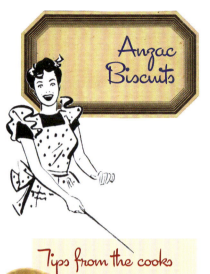

Anzac Biscuits

Recipe

1 cup (90 g) rolled oats
1 cup (150 g) plain flour
1 cup (220 g) firmly packed brown sugar
½ cup (40 g) desiccated coconut
125 g butter
2 tablespoons golden syrup
1 tablespoon water
½ teaspoon bicarbonate of soda

Preheat oven to 160 °C/140 °C fan-forced. Grease oven trays; line with baking paper.

Combine oats, sifted flour, sugar and coconut in large bowl. Combine butter, syrup and the water in small saucepan, stir over low heat until smooth; stir in soda. Stir into dry ingredients.

Roll level tablespoons of mixture into balls; place about 5 cm apart on trays, flatten slightly. Bake about 20 minutes; cool on trays.

MAKES 25 BISCUITS.

*Reprinted with permission from The Australian Women's Weekly cookbook *Old-fashioned Favourites*, ACP Books, RRP $12.95, available from selected newsagents, supermarkets and online at www.acpbooks.com.au

Tips from the cooks

- The biscuits should be quite flat when they are cooked properly. If they are still slightly peaky in the middle, leave them in the oven for a bit longer, or they will have a soft centre.
- Cool the biscuits on a flat surface but not a wire rack if they are going to be shown.

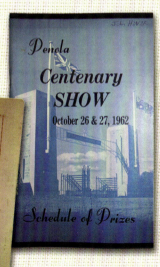

Above: Ploughing the former showground, now the Penola Primary School oval, c. 1920s (JH)

Left: Premier Thomas Playford opens the new showground gates, 1952 (JH)

Below, left: Farm implements at the Penola Show, 1905 (SLSA: B 33749)

Below: Penola show book covers, 1950 and 1962 (JH)

PINNAROO
Chocolate Layer Cake

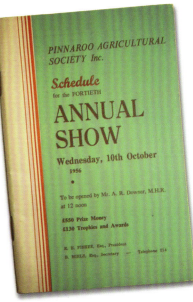

For Dorothy Barker cooking is a little bit like dancing. 'I learnt to cook by helping Mum. It was just natural, like dancing. I never really learnt to dance, my dad just got us on the floor and we danced,' she says.

Dorothy grew up in the South Australian Mallee, moving from place to place as a child, with her father working as a farm labourer. 'After every harvest he used to have to get another job, so after every harvest we had to pack up and move to another farmhouse.' She remembers that the kitchens in most houses were 'add-ons', attached to the back, and that her mother, Ann Mill, was an excellent cook despite the often temperamental ovens she had to use.

Ann started to compete at the Pinnaroo Show after the family moved into town during World War II, when Dorothy was about twelve. In later years, her older sister, Jean (Mickan) competed too and Jean and Ann both went on to convene the cookery section. Dorothy didn't start cooking for competition until she was about 35 and the youngest of her four children was about five years old. 'They kept me a bit busy,' she says. She later worked part-time as a cook at the local hospital and pub, which she says was 'like cooking at home but on a bigger scale'.

All three women often competed against each other, which Dorothy says was a lot of fun. More often than not they used to 'tussle' over first place with their velvety, light chocolate layer cakes and ribbon cakes made using the same basic recipe. The chocolate version is a family favourite, but Dorothy hasn't made it for competition since her sister died in 2003. 'I lost heart and gave up on it,' she admits. 'The recipe is out of my mother's book. I don't know where she got it from but it's such an easy cake to make and that's why she passed it on.'

One of the few remaining mid-week shows in South Australia, Pinnaroo held its first show in 1910. The spring event is

Opposite page, top: Dorothy Barker (VS) **Opposite page, bottom:** Pinnaroo show book cover, 1956

Top: Pinnaroo Agricultural Society Show: an exhibit of local women's handicraft work, c. 1926 (SLSA: B 18674)

Above: Horses at the Pinnaroo Show, c. 1928 (SLSA: B 17298)

Opposite page: Waiting for the official opening of show day, 2007

always held on a Wednesday, which was a popular day for many early shows, and is well supported by the local community, with local schools taking a holiday to participate.

Today it also incorporates a field day with displays of agricultural equipment and information for local farmers.

Recipe

1 cup plain flour
1 tablespoon cocoa powder
1 teaspoon cream of tartar
1 tablespoon cornflour
$1/3$ teaspoon salt
3 eggs
1 cup castor sugar
1 cup milk
1 tablespoon butter (or margarine)
$1/2$ teaspoon bicarbonate of soda

Butter icing

1 tablespoon cocoa powder
2 tablespoons hot water
2 cups icing sugar
1 tablespoon butter

Tips from the cook

- Concentrate and have everything organised before you start. Follow the method in the exact order and work quickly once you have added the bicarbonate of soda.
- Make sure the eggs and butter are at room temperature.
- Try greasing your cake pans with copha instead of oil or butter.
- The cake is lovely filled with berries and whipped cream when you make it for home.

Preheat the oven to moderate (180 °C in a conventional electric oven).

Grease two deep 18 cm round cake pans and line the bottoms with greaseproof or baking paper.

Sift together the flour, cocoa, cream of tartar, cornflour and salt at least four times.

Put the eggs and sugar in a large bowl and beat on a high speed with electric hand-held beaters or a mix-master until light and fluffy.

Put the milk and butter in a small saucepan and bring to the boil.

Gently fold the dry ingredients into the egg mixture.

Add the soda to the milk. As soon as it has dissolved and the milk is fizzing, tip it into the cake mixture and stir gently with a spoon until smooth. Use a spatula to make sure all the mixture from the bottom and sides of the bowl is incorporated. The final mixture should be quite thin in consistency.

Divide the mixture evenly between the two cake pans and bake for 20 to 25 minutes; the cakes should be firm and springy to the touch and just starting to come away from the edge of the pans.

Remove the cakes from the oven and let them sit for a few minutes before loosening the sides very carefully with a knife and turning them out to cool.

Use butter icing to join the layers together and decorate the top once the cakes are cold.

Butter icing

Dissolve the cocoa in 2 tablespoons of hot water. Blend the cocoa mixture with the icing sugar and butter, adding a little more water if required until the icing is smooth and spreadable.

Variation: Ribbon cake

You will need to make three separate batches of this mixture and use a slightly larger pan (20 cm round cake pan). Make the chocolate layer as above. For the pink layer, substitute the cocoa for a tablespoon of cornflour, and add a few drops of strawberry red food colouring, one drop at a time until you get a rich pink colour (the cake will lose a little bit of colour with cooking). For the plain layer, substitute the cocoa for a tablespoon of cornflour. Join the layers with raspberry jam, placing the chocolate layer on the bottom, the pink layer in the middle, and the plain layer on top. Finish with butter icing.

Tips from the judges

- The cake should be well risen and the top smooth and flat, with the icing and filling applied neatly. It should have a rich chocolate colour and a fine texture.
- The layers need to be even and made from the same mixture.

PORT ELLIOT
Grandma's Chocolate Fudge Cake

Top: Hannah Ogilvie

Above: Hannah as a young child cooking with her grandmother, Neta Davies Hewitt (OF)

Hannah Ogilvie has a special legacy. Some years ago her great grandmother sat down and put together printed folders for all her descendants, capturing family recipes and the little insights she has garnered over a lifetime of cooking. Now living at Point Pass north of Eudunda, Neta Davies Hewitt started competing at shows in 1928 at the age of twelve. At 24, she began her long career of judging at country shows and, eventually, at the Royal Adelaide Show.

Her great granddaughter loved cooking almost from the time she could walk. Hannah began 'official' cooking lessons with Neta when she was eight, as part of home schooling. Every Wednesday afternoon they would work together to perfect one savoury dish and one sweet, later eating them for dinner. As guidance, Neta made careful handwritten notes, which are among Hannah's most treasured possessions. The teenager from Victor Harbor is already an experienced show cook with many first prizes to her name in both junior and adult sections, and gives up part of her school holidays to work as a steward for the Southern Agriculture Society's show at Port Elliot.

The society actively encourages young people like Hannah to become involved in the show, helping to ensure its future. Like many show societies operating in metropolitan and peri-urban areas, the organisation also believes it has a major role to play in bringing together town and rural communities and raising awareness about agriculture. Every Olympic year, it awards an Excellence in Primary Industries Award to celebrate achievements in the primary sector. The endeavour would have pleased the founders of the show, which started in 1869 with livestock exhibits 'quite equal in quality to any that has taken place in the colony', according to the *Victor Harbor Times*. The event moved between Goolwa, Middleton, Port Elliot and Port Victor before taking up permanent residence at dedicated grounds at Port Elliot in 1889, and has long drawn 'influential agriculturalists' and state dignitaries.

There is little mention of cookery in newspaper reports of the

Tips from the judges

- Check the schedule carefully for instructions about cake pan size.
- Never stand the cake on a rack to cool – rack marks on the bottom are a major no-no for show cooking.

Left: W.P. Dunk, justice of the peace and businessman from Milang attending the Mount Pleasant agricultural show, 1914. According to a special feature on the history of the Port Elliot Show, published by the *Victor Harbor Times*, he attended every one of the first 50 shows organised by the Southern Agricultural Society and was known as the 'Grand Old Man of the South' (SLSA: PRG 280/1/13/154)

Below: A show book advertisement for Bennett and Fisher Ltd

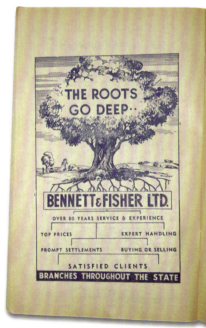

show until 1877: 'Perhaps one of the best lines shown was some homemade bread, of which there were no less than six entries; and right good substantial bread it look, too – well risen and well baked.' Bread remains on the schedule today, with classes for both homemade and machine-made versions.

But for Hannah the focus is, more often than not, the chocolate cake classes. She uses her great grandmother's recipe, which is also a family favourite.

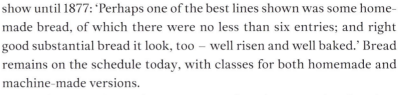

Recipe

60 g butter
1 cup sugar
1 egg
1 tablespoon cocoa powder

$1\frac{1}{2}$ cups SR flour
$\frac{1}{2}$ teaspoon bicarbonate of soda
$\frac{1}{2}$ cup milk
$\frac{1}{4}$ cup boiling water

Preheat the oven to moderate (180 °C in a conventional electric oven).

Grease a 20 cm ring pan. (Alternatively grease and line two log pans or a deep 20 cm round cake pan.)

Beat the butter and sugar until light and fluffy. Beat in the egg.

Sift together the cocoa and flour. In a separate bowl, blend the soda and milk.

Add the flour and the milk mixtures alternatively to the butter and sugar and stir until smooth. Add the boiling water last.

Pour the mixture evenly into the prepared pan and bake for 30 minutes.

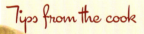

Tips from the cook

- Always sift the cocoa to get rid of any lumps.
- According to Hannah, free-range eggs produce a better texture.
- Adding boiling water makes the cake moist, which scores points with the judges, and the cake seems to hold together better.

Opposite page: Junior cookery entries at the Port Elliot Show

Above: Hannah Ogilvie helping out as a steward, with cookery judge Joan Elsegood and steward Margaret Dent

Left: First prize winner in a bread class at the Port Elliot Show

PORT LINCOLN
Fruit and Nut Loaf

People travelled far and wide to eat Heather Nettle's homemade pies, pasties and sausage rolls when she baked for the general store at Wangary, on the southern tip of Eyre Peninsula. 'We used to have people from Adelaide ring up to order a heap to take back home with them when they were visiting,' she recalls. Heather and her late husband ran the store for eighteen years after moving from Adelaide, and later set up a biscuit shop in Port Lincoln.

These days she cooks for community stalls and works as a volunteer at the popular Coffin Bay Yacht Club. Heather always prepares a few entries for the Port Lincoln Show, which has taken on a new lease of life since moving to the town's racecourse in 2007, about 100 years after the first event.

For Heather, the joy of show cooking lies in the camaraderie. She loves working alongside other people and talking with fellow cooks as well as judges to pick up tips. 'You do it just to be there and the more people that enter the better it makes the show,' she says. Heather is both a practical and an inventive cook, adapting recipes to suit what is at hand, a skill she picked up from her mother:

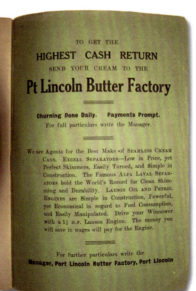

She learnt how to make something out of nothing like a lot of women . . . Dad was in the highways and she used to go out to the highway camps too and cook rough. She cooked on a three-burner kerosene stove with an oven that fitted on top of that.

This fruit and nut loaf recipe is one of Heather's own, developed through trial and error, using different core ingredients than traditional loaves.

Recipe

½ cup sultanas
½ cup dried apricots, pineapple or fruit medley, chopped
1 level teaspoon bicarbonate of soda
1 cup boiling water
2 tablespoons butter
¾ cup sugar
1 egg, well beaten
1½ cups SR flour
½ cup plain flour
½ cup chopped nuts

Put the sultanas and other dried fruit in a bowl. Add the soda to the boiling water and pour over the fruit; let stand for about half an hour.

Preheat the oven to moderate (180 °C in a conventional electric oven) and arrange a shelf so there is room to place the two tins, standing up in the middle of the oven. Grease thoroughly the insides of two cylindrical nut roll tins with butter or margarine.

Cream the butter and sugar until light and fluffy. Beat in the egg. Sift in the SR and plain flour, and add the undrained fruit and nuts. Stir until combined.

Carefully spoon the mixture into the tins. Stand them up on a tray and place them in the oven. Bake for about 40 minutes.

Remove the tins from the oven and let them stand for 5 to 10 minutes so the loaves are easier to remove.

Tips from the cook

- Use light brown sugar instead of plain white sugar, and any combination of fruit and nuts you like.
- If you don't have the correct nut roll tins, use fruit tins, with the labels removed, and make ends out of alfoil, tied on firmly with butcher's twine.
- Don't use oil to grease the tins.

Tips from the judges

- Make sure the fruit and nuts are evenly cut and distributed.
- The loaf should have clean, undamaged sides and a close, firm texture while being moist and soft.
- Judges have different preferences for whether the loaf should be flat at both ends, or domed at one end. It can take some practice in judging the amount of mixture to put into the tin to achieve flat ends. Do not overfill the tin; it should be about two-thirds full, depending on the recipe.

Opposite page, top: Heather Nettle making her fruit and nut loaf

Opposite page, bottom: A show book advertisement for the Port Lincoln Butter Factory, 1918 (YFAHS)

QUORN
Moderator's Slice

'Everything eatable which the most fastidious could desire' was served at a special dinner to celebrate the inaugural Quorn Show in 1880, according to a report in the Port Augusta *Dispatch*:

From 8.00 am on Tuesday, horses, vehicles and pedestrians thronged the township, and by the time the special train arrived from Pt. Augusta the township must have contained 1200 to 1500 visitors, and as a day of wind and dust, hurry bustle and confusion, will long be remembered in Quorn by both visitors and residents.

Shows continued periodically until the Depression, starting up again after World War II. Among the many volunteers who keep the event going today is cookery steward Valmai Roeby, a local born and bred, who has been competing in shows with great success for more than 30 years. She started entering flowers, then moved on to knitting, and later decided to have a go at cooking after working in the section. 'I was a steward first and if you stand there and listen, you can learn a lot from what the judges say,' she advises.

Although Valmai didn't go 'hammer and tongs' initially, she went on to become an enthusiastic competitor, winning the Quorn cookery aggregate most years from 1989. 'My [late] husband would say "it must be showtime or something is happening at the bowls because the house is full of cakes and biscuits",' she recalls.

Her Moderator's Slice recipe came from a friend and formed part of a prizewinning collection entered in the unbaked slices class. 'Rich but very yummy,' says the cook.

Recipe

Base
2 tablespoons cocoa powder
1 cup icing sugar
1 cup desiccated coconut
4 cups cornflakes
250 g copha, melted

Filling
200 ml sweetened condensed milk
$\frac{1}{4}$ cup brown sugar
2 tablespoons golden syrup
60 g butter
1 teaspoon vanilla essence

Grease and line a 19 x 29 cm slice pan.

To make the base, combine the cocoa, icing sugar, coconut and cornflakes in a large bowl. Pour over the melted copha and mix well. Press half the mixture into the prepared pan and place in the refrigerator while you prepare the filling.

To make the filling, place the condensed milk, sugar, golden syrup, butter and vanilla in a saucepan and bring gently to the boil, stirring continuously. Keep stirring the mixture while it simmers for 3 minutes. Cool the filling and then pour it over the base.

To finish the slice, top it with the remaining base mixture and put it in the refrigerator to set. Cut the slice into squares when firm and store them in the refrigerator.

Opposite page, top: Valmai Roeby
Opposite page, bottom: The Quorn showground

Tips from the cook
- The base only needs to be left in the refrigerator for as long as it takes to make and cool the filling.
- When applying the final layer, just scatter it evenly over the filling and press it down very lightly.

Tips from the judges
- Make sure all the slices in a collection are neatly and evenly cut, and that they complement each other.
- This slice should be crunchy in texture.

RENMARK
Orange Cake

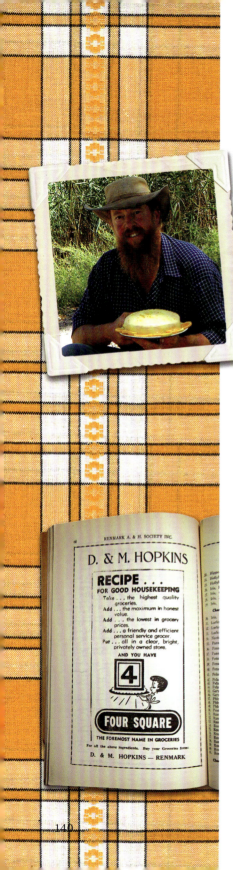

You would be hard-pushed to describe Paul Hansen as a typical show cook. Born and bred at historic Kulcurna Station near Lake Victoria, Paul counts taxidermy, song writing and photography among his many skills. He also makes a mean orange cake. Although he has been known to whip up a six-course dinner party for 80 people to raise money for the local gun club, his training for the task was far from conventional. 'I work away a lot in mustering camps and I am normally head cook and bottle washer for eight to ten people, but there is not a lot of cake cooking,' he says.

Like many country show towns, Renmark has introduced a men's only cake competition in recent years to generate fresh interest in cookery. The contest is fierce in this Riverland version, which celebrates local produce by insisting the blokes make an orange cake using a recipe provided. Paul won first prize in 2007 with a cake decorated by torchlight on the bonnet of his ute; he had to do it at the last minute after being held up organising entries for the wool section, which he convenes. 'I don't take it too seriously. I just came in after work one evening, threw everything into a bowl, mixed it up, put it in the oven and off we went,' he says. 'I just did what they said I had to do in the show book.'

Paul has also been known to enter taxidermy in the craft section. He studied the relatively lost art by correspondence about eighteen years ago, and has sometimes been asked by wildlife services to help preserve animals and birds for display. 'I don't know what got me into it,' he confesses. 'But I don't do heads on walls. I am more interested in preservation.'

Through his volunteering and competing at the show, Paul is following a long-standing family tradition. His great grandfather exhibited at the very first Renmark Show, and the society is due to hold its 100th event in 2010. It comes at a time when the show society is gaining a new lease of life, winning a Community Event of the Year award and drawing more patrons. Among the most popular attractions are the vintage tractor and stationery engine displays, a ute muster, native animal displays, and a giant sandpit for the children.

Top: Paul Hansen (BH)   **Left:** Show book advertisement – good housekeeping
Opposite page: Paul Hansen on the banks of the River Murray at Kulcurna Station (BH)

Orange Cake

Recipe

85 g butter (or margarine), softened
3 eggs (50 g each)
1¼ cups SR flour, sifted
½ cup castor sugar
90 ml orange juice
grated rind of one navel orange

Preheat the oven to moderate (180 °C in a conventional electric oven).

Grease a 20 cm round cake pan, and line the base.

Put the butter, eggs, flour, sugar, orange juice and rind in a large bowl and beat with an electric mixer for about 3 minutes. Pour the mixture into the prepared cake pan and bake for 30 to 40 minutes, until golden brown and firm to the touch.

Tips from the cook

- Put a bit of effort into presentation if you want to impress the judges.

Tips from the judges

- Decorate the cake with orange-flavoured icing.
- Too much acid will cause the cake to collapse so don't overdo the orange juice.
- The top should be smooth and lightly rounded, without any cracks. It should not be sticky, which can be caused by too cool an oven or not beating the sugar enough.
- The texture should be fine, moist and even without any holes.

Left: Decorating the orange cake (BH)

Below: Renmark show book covers, 1958 and 2007, and a show book advertisement for the Renmark Fruit Growers Cooperative

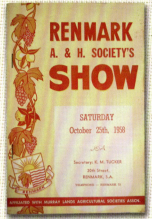

STRATHALBYN
Carrot Cake

There are some hazards in show cooking that catch even the most meticulous cooks by surprise. Take the year that Rex Liebelt walked into the hall of an un-named show to see if he had won any prizes and noticed his carrot cake looked a bit odd. Apparently, a stray cat had discovered the cake sitting on a bench and licked off the icing.

Rex has a well-deserved reputation for baking outstanding cakes and his genuine love of country shows. He has served as secretary of the Southern Country Shows Association and on committees for five separate societies, and was chairman of the steering committee that revived the Mount Barker Show after a recess of 26 years.

He was introduced to the world of shows in 1979 when he started showing poultry. 'Then I started looking through show books and I thought I would do other things too,' he recalls. Rex liked baking cakes when young so he decided to give the cookery section a try, although it took a while to start winning on a regular basis. 'I wasn't doing all that well with the recipes I had so I looked up books and tried new ones until I found something that worked.' He doesn't remember there being a lot of other men competing when he started but has found there are quite a few now.

Rex is best known for his chocolate, banana, orange, carrot and butterfly cakes, and recently added beer cake to his repertoire. His prizewinning carrot cake recipe is taken from a cookbook published by St Marks Lutheran Church in Dubbo, and given to him by his parents in 1992. 'I follow the recipe every time I bake the cake and it always turns out well,' he says.

One of the oldest show societies in the state, Strathalbyn held its first show in 1856. The event quickly grew in size and stature, with a report of the 10th event noting that 'nothing ever shown before equalled the extent and quality' of the fruit exhibits, and the vegetables featured 'cabbages with hearts as hard as bullets but crisp as a tender lettuce'. The 1900 show boasted 'some nicely got up cakes' although the apples were a 'miserable lot'. The spring event continues to grow in popularity, with the 2007 show setting a new record for gate takings despite the equine flu outbreak causing horse events to be cancelled.

Tips from the cook

- You can divide the mixture into two log tins, or make one 18 cm round cake. The round cake takes twice as long to cook – about 2 hours.
- Rex beats this cake mixture by hand, using a large metal spoon.
- The cake freezes well, without the topping.
- The topping can be kept in the refrigerator and spread without warming.

Tips from the judges

- The cake should be well risen with straight, neat sides and a slightly round or flat top. There should be evenly distributed specks of carrot and spice showing.
- The cake should have a fine, even and moist texture; it should not be crumbly.

Recipe

2 cups sugar
$1\frac{1}{2}$ cups vegetable oil
3 cups coarsely grated carrot
4 eggs
2 cups plain flour
2 teaspoons bicarbonate of soda
1 teaspoon salt
2 teaspoons cinnamon
1 teaspoon vanilla essence
$\frac{1}{2}$ cup chopped walnuts

Topping

60 g cream cheese
125 g icing sugar
30 g butter
$\frac{1}{2}$ teaspoon vanilla essence

Preheat the oven to moderate (180 °C in a conventional electric oven).

Grease and line two log tins or an 18 cm round cake pan.

In a large bowl, beat together the sugar and oil until mixed thoroughly. Add the carrot and eggs, continuing to beat well. Sift the flour, soda, salt and cinnamon into the carrot mixture. Add the vanilla and the nuts.

Pour the mixture into the tins and bake for 1 hour if using the log pans or about 2 hours if using the round pan – or until golden brown and firm to the touch. Allow to stand for a few minutes before turning out of the tins to cool.

Topping

Beat together the cream cheese, icing sugar, butter and vanilla and spread evenly over the cake.

Opposite page, top: Rex Liebelt and his prizewinning carrot cake

Opposite page, bottom: Windmill display stands at an agricultural show in Strathalbyn, 1914 (SLSA: PRG 280/1/10/52)

SWAN REACH
Jenny's Grape Jam

Fires, floods and war have taken their toll on the Swan Reach Show over the years, but the event soldiers on with an occasional recess to give the community time to regroup. As the *Swan Express* put it in 1978: 'The changes have been drastic . . . However, the spirit of the show remains essentially the same – the aura of competition and striving, and the family togetherness.'

A paddle-steamer carried visitors along the River Murray to an agricultural show at Swan Reach in 1899 but the first official show organised by the local agricultural society was not held until two years later. The legendary floods of 1956 destroyed all the show records, but newspaper reports tell us Miss E. Brecht won the prize for the best 'luncheon in a basket'.

The 1917 show was abandoned because of the high state of the river. The event went into recess during World War II, and was set to make a come back when fire destroyed the hall in 1946. It did not resume until eight years later when a new stone pavilion was used for the first time. The show continued to be a major local drawcard during the 1970s and 1980s, and the society celebrated its 90th show in 2003.

Helping out these days as treasurer is local cook Jenny Nuske, who is known for her preserves. A cook by trade as well as inclination, Jenny worked at the Swan Reach pub for many years and now turns out meals at the historic Pretoria Hotel in Mannum. 'I have allergies to things so I had to learn how to do my own preserves,' Jenny says. Sugared almonds and cucumber pickles are among her favourites, together with this prizewinning recipe for grape jam.

Recipe

3 kg grapes, any variety
1 cup water
sugar
juice of 2 lemons
½ cup port (optional)

Wash the grapes and remove the stalks. Place in a preserving pan with one cup of water. Boil gently until the grapes are very soft, the juice flows and any seeds start to float.

Skim off the seeds and then sieve the mixture through a colander.

Return the fruit to the pan and add 1 cup of sugar for every cup of pulp. Stir in the lemon juice and, if desired, the port.

Boil quickly until the jam starts to set. Pour it into sterilised jars and seal.

Tips from the cook

- Use any variety or combination of green and black grapes.
- Cooking times for the fruit may vary considerably – from 10 to 30 minutes. If the fruit is very ripe it will soften faster but contains less pectin so you might want to use more lemon juice, or try making it with jam setting sugar, available in supermarkets, which contains added pectin.
- The grapes can be cooked stalks and all, and then sieved through a mouli to eliminate the stalks and seeds before adding the sugar.
- The jam has reached setting point when it drops thickly from a spoon. Alternatively, place a small spoonful on a cold saucer, wait a few moments for it to cool and then push it with your finger. The jam is set when it wrinkles.

Tips from the judges

- Always exhibit the correct number, variety, jars and seals according to the schedule.
- Jars should be filled to within 1 cm of the top.

Left: Machinery demonstrations at an early agricultural show in Swan Reach, 1899 (SRM)

Opposite page, top: Jenny Nuske

Opposite page, bottom: Show book cover from the 1940s (SRM)

TANUNDA
German Yeast Cake

Spend a little time in the Barossa Valley and you soon learn that making a German yeast cake, or streusel kuchen, is a highly respected art form – and every cook has their own way of doing it. Traditionally, people learnt how to make them working alongside their mother or grandmother, often using a commercial kuchen essence, which is now difficult to come by, and a secret recipe handed down through the generations but kept strictly within the family.

According to champion Tanunda cooks and show judges Esma Hein and Joan Lindner, there is no substitute for learning first-hand. 'You have to know what it should look like before you go on to the next step,' Joan says. 'It's alright to tell people but there are so many variables,' adds Esma. 'Every flour is different so you may have to have more or less milk, and the size of the eggs affects it too, then there is the temperature on the day and the humidity.'

Friendly rivals for many years, the two women have an outstanding record in competitive cooking. Joan won the Royal Adelaide Show cookery section aggregate more than fifteen times in succession after starting her show career at Tanunda in the late 1960s. 'I know I did seven entries the first year and after that it was full on. The most I ever did was 52 classes in Adelaide and that was 83 recipes,' she says. Looking back at the huge endeavour, she confesses it was 'plain stupidity'. Esma has won aggregate trophies in Adelaide a few times in both cookery and preserves, as well as the State Genoa Cake Competition; and she is well known at the Barossa Farmers Market for her baked goods and preserves. She grew up on a farm near Murray Bridge and started competing in 1948. 'My sister

Top: Esma Hein and Joan Lindner
Left: Show book advertisement for Hardy's Tintara Wines
Right: Show book advertisement for Fauldings Essences

was putting things in the show, and when she got married and left home I thought if she can do it I can do it too,' Esma says. 'I only put three or four entries in but I got a trophy and I thought this is all right . . . I still am quite hooked. It just gets to you.'

Although neither woman competes much these days, cookery entries are on the rise at the increasingly popular Tanunda Show, held in March during vintage. As part of its endeavour to celebrate the Barossa Valley's rich German heritage, the show hosts South Australian championships for dill cucumbers, pickled onions, rote grütze and, of course, German yeast cake. The following recipe is based on one provided by the family of Marie Schultz from Laura Blocks, who won first prize with it at Tanunda in 1978. There are three main stages – setting the sponge (making the yeast mixture), making the kuchen (kneading and proofing the dough), and making the streusel topping (added just before baking).

Recipe

Sponge (yeast mixture)

25 g compressed yeast
1 cup full-cream milk, warm
$1\frac{1}{4}$ cups plain flour
1 tablespoon sugar

Mix together the yeast, milk, flour and sugar until it is smooth and looks like thick cream. Pour the mixture into a saucepan, and put the lid on. Set the saucepan in a warm place for about 10 minutes or until it starts to froth and rise, developing a good head.

Kuchen

1.125 kg (7 cups) unbleached bread flour
1 teaspoon nutmeg
$\frac{1}{2}$ teaspoon cinnamon
$\frac{1}{2}$ teaspoon mace
$\frac{1}{3}$ cup sultanas
315 g ($1\frac{1}{4}$ cups) sugar
4 eggs
2 cups milk
2 teaspoons kuchen essence (or 1 teaspoon each of lemon essence and vanilla essence)
265 g butter, melted
melted butter, extra

In a large bowl, sift together the flour, nutmeg, cinnamon and mace; stir in the sultanas and sugar. In a smaller bowl, beat together the eggs and milk; stir in the kuchen. Add the egg mixture to the dry ingredients, then pour in the melted butter and the sponge mixture. Using your hands, mix it into a soft, sticky dough. Knead dough until it is smooth and satiny in texture (about 5 to 8 minutes). Put the dough in a very

Tips from the cooks

When setting the sponge:
- Mix the yeast and sugar together first to help dissolve the yeast and avoid the mixture going lumpy; then add the flour. The time it takes to set will depend on the yeast and the temperature of your kitchen on the day.
- Make sure the milk is warm (but not hot) to help activate the yeast.
- If you set the sponge and it doesn't rise, don't go any further. Start again.

Making the kuchen:
- Esma mixes her kuchen in a large, wide 9 litre stockpot.
- Make your own kuchen essence using lemon and vanilla essences in equal portions.
- Esma measures flour and sugar with a cup, not by weight, and uses mace but not nutmeg in the flavourings.
- You don't have to use sultanas – Joan finds the texture is better without them.
- Make sure the melted butter is cool before you add the eggs to avoid cooking them. Joan pours the milk onto the butter before adding it to the dry ingredients to make sure the butter isn't too hot.
- If the mixture is too slack, add a bit more flour. The dough should be nice and pliant, and a lot moister than bread dough. Mix it with your hand so you can tell when it's the right consistency; it should come away in strings and then drop off your fingers.

Tips from the cooks

- Don't use so much grease to prepare the trays that you end up 'frying' the cakes.
- You should be aiming for a kuchen that is about 3 cm high when it's cooked, so pat the dough out on the slide until it is about 1.5 cm thick. Coat your hands with a little bit of margarine or butter so the dough doesn't stick to your fingers.
- Keeping the yeast warm is critical. Once it's on the trays, Esma stands them on an electric blanket, which she spreads over her kitchen bench.
- When the dough starts to rise on the slides, 'you have to run', warns Joan. Timing from this point is critical.
- Instead of brushing the cakes with butter before adding the streusel, try using a thin layer of thick cream.
- You may need to turn the yeast cakes about halfway through the cooking time to ensure they are even.

Making the streusel:
- Joan and Esma use a ratio of ¾ cup of sugar to every cup of flour for the topping.
- Add a bit more butter if you find the streusel is not binding together properly; it has to be lumpy so it doesn't fall off the cake.
- Esma prefers to use only cinnamon as flavouring for the streusel but it's all about personal preference – experiment.

large bowl, cover it with a tea towel and set in a warm place to rise – the dough needs to double in size, which may take about 2 hours.

Grease four large oven trays or slab pans; you can also use Swiss roll or lamington pans.

Divide the dough into four pieces and pat them out onto the oven trays or slab pans. To do this, drop once piece of dough in the middle of each tray and work it out towards the edges, trying to make it as even as possible.

Put the dough in a warm place and let it rise again for about 20 to 30 minutes. While it is rising, preheat the oven to moderate (180 °C in a conventional electric oven) and make the streusel.

Once the dough has risen, brush it with melted butter and scatter the streusel evenly over the top. Bake in a moderate oven for 20 to 30 minutes, or until golden.

Streusel

625 g (4 cups) plain flour
470 g (2 cups) sugar
440 g butter
1 teaspoon cinnamon
½ teaspoon nutmeg
¼ teaspoon mace
12 drops vanilla essence

Rub all the ingredients together until lumps form.
MAKES ABOUT 4 LARGE YEAST CAKES.

Above: Sir Day Bosanquet, Governor of South Australia, seated with judges and other guests at a Tanunda agricultural show, 1912 (SLSA: PRG 280/1/6/319)

Above: First prize tickets from the Tanunda Show

Tips from the judge

- The yeast cake must be baked evenly, with no burnt edges, and the topping must adhere to the cake.
- The texture should be finer than bread, with no large holes caused by air bubbles.
- The cake should have a subtle flavour, with a delicate balance of essence and spice.

URAIDLA
Apple Squares

One of Jean Evans's earliest memories of the Uraidla Show is her father polishing up the horns of a Jersey cow before leading it down the road to compete in the livestock section. Her family took up land in the beautiful Piccadilly Valley in the 1840s and were involved in the show from its beginnings in 1883. The autumn event set out to showcase local produce from 'the finest fruit, flower and vegetable producing district of the colony'. A highlight for many years was the show luncheon, with local women turning out 'famous' feasts in a small dirt-floored kitchen while plum puddings 'reheated on an outside fire made of big stones and two iron bars'.

Jean's first contribution to cooking at the show was a collection of ten biscuits, made when she was about fourteen years old. She learnt to cook from her mother, but was influenced by relatives on both sides of the family who were professional cooks and bakers. Jean worked on Sundays for her uncle, Bert Dyer, who was a baker and ran a cafe in Stirling. 'I love cooking. I really love cooking, I do. I have always loved it,' she enthuses. 'Cooking is never a chore.'

Jean is well known in the district for her prizewinning apple squares, which are something of an Adelaide Hills institution. The recipe came from her mother-in-law, Mona Evans, an Edinburgh war bride who came to Australia after World War I. Jean's husband Bob can remember his mother making them when he was young and

suspects she brought the recipe from Scotland where her grandmother was a cook on a large country estate. In Australia 'Grandma Evans', Mona, took the apple squares to any community event she attended. Jean continues the tradition to this day, baking them in an old square pan inherited from her mother-in-law and made from the lid of a Mottram's flour tin.

Opposite page, top: Jean Evans

Opposite page, bottom: Members of an early Uraidla Society Ladies Committee (USHFSI)

Above, left: Judging cakes at the Uraidla Show

Above, top: Uraidla show book cover, 1988

Above, below: Judging jams at the Uraidla show

Left: A volunteer steward recording results

Recipe

Filling

4 to 5 medium Granny Smith apples, peeled, quartered and chopped
1 tablespoon water
1 tablespoon sugar

Pastry

125 g butter
$\frac{1}{2}$ cup castor sugar
1 egg
$1\frac{1}{4}$ cups SR flour
pinch of salt
$\frac{1}{4}$ cup cornflour

Preheat the oven to moderate (180 °C in a conventional electric oven). Grease and line a 23 cm square slab pan.

To make the filling, place the prepared apples in a saucepan with the water and sugar. Simmer gently until soft. Drain to remove all excess moisture and set aside to cool. Mash the apples to create a rough puree.

To make the pastry, cream the butter and sugar until light and fluffy, and the sugar is dissolved. Add the egg, and beat again until light and fluffy. Sift together the flour, salt and cornflour. Add the dry ingredients slowly to the butter mixture, mixing together with a knife to form a ball. Knead the dough until it is smooth and pliable.

To make the slice, divide the pastry in half. Roll out one half on a lightly floured surface, so it is roughly large enough to cover the bottom of the pan. Place the pastry in the pan and gently press to make sure it fits into the sides and corners. Spread the cold stewed apples evenly over the pastry.

Roll out the remaining dough so that it is large enough to cover the pan. Use the rolling pin to lift the pastry and place it over the apples. Alternatively, fold the pastry into three layers. Place one edge against the edge of the pan and unfold the pastry over the apples. Trim the pastry to fit.

Cook the slice for about 25 minutes. Reduce the temperature to moderately slow and cook for another 10 minutes, until crisp on top.

Turn out onto a wire rack, so that the top is face down. If necessary, remove the paper and return to the oven on the rack for another 5 minutes to brown the bottom. Turn onto a metal tray to cool. Dust with icing sugar and cut into squares.

Tips from the cook

- Prepare the filling first so it is cold when you need it. Adjust the amount of apples you use to suit personal taste.
- Use a standard (large) egg to make the pastry. If the egg is too large the dough will be too 'wet'.
- The dough will be easier to handle if you keep it cold. Try putting it in the fridge for about 30 minutes after kneading.
- Use cornflour to flour the board and rolling pin when you are working the pastry.
- Serve with cream or ice cream for dessert. The slice keeps well in the deep freeze.

Tips from the judges

- Take care not to burn or discolour the apples.
- Don't use pieces taken from the outside edge.

Left and below: Making apple squares in Grandma Evans's original tin

WHYALLA
Cream Puffs

Making cream puffs is second nature for Evelyn Parkes, who turns them out in their hundreds for family, community groups and local residents wanting treats for a special occasion.

A resident of Whyalla since she was a small child, Evelyn lined up to compete at the town's very first show in 1971 and she has been there ever since, providing catering for volunteers and officials as well as entering competitive sections. She is following in family footsteps – her grandfather was a professional baker and her mother used to help him make pasties to sell at local hotels every weekend. 'I came from a family of seven girls and one boy, so we learnt to cook,' Evelyn says matter-of-factly. 'My aunty was a beautiful puff pastry cook so I learnt that from her.'

She thinks her original cream puff recipe may have come from her mother, 'but you learn your own techniques as you go along,' she says. Evelyn obviously has a deft touch – her puffs have won best exhibit more than once, and she has brought home ribbons from Kimba, Port Augusta and Adelaide for her pasties and sausage rolls.

A relative newcomer to the show calendar, the two-day Whyalla event draws about 25,000 people from as far as Port Lincoln. Volunteers work hard to constantly improve facilities for the show, which has developed a strong reputation for its top-class entertainment program, commercial displays and horse events.

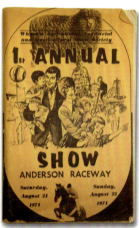

Top: Evelyn Parkes

Left: A Golden North advertisement from an early Whyalla show book, cover of the first Whyalla show book, and the 2006 show book cover (WSSI)

Opposite page: Making cream puffs

Recipe

1 cup hot water
125 g butter (or margarine)
1 cup SR flour
4 eggs, unbeaten
whipped cream (or crème patisserie)

Preheat the oven to hot (220 °C in a conventional electric oven). Line an oven tray with baking paper.

Put the water and butter in a large saucepan and bring to the boil. Sift in the flour. Take from the heat and stir to a smooth paste. Transfer the mixture to a large bowl and allow it to cool.

Add the eggs and beat for 5 minutes, using hand-held beaters or a mix-master set at a moderate speed.

Place rounded dessertspoons of mixture on the prepared tray, allowing room for expansion. Bake for 25 to 30 minutes, until crisp to the touch and golden brown (they should sound hollow when you tap the bottom).

Once they are cold, cut them in half and fill with whipped cream or crème patisserie.
MAKES 14 TO 16 CREAM PUFFS.

Tips from the cook

- Make sure the eggs are fresh; if you are mixing by hand add them one at a time.
- Turn the oven tray after 20 minutes so the cream puffs brown evenly.
- One of the most common mistakes is not cooking them enough – make sure they are dry inside when you take them out of the oven.
- They will store well in an airtight container or the deep freeze; put them back in the oven to crisp up when you need them.
- For competition, use an old baker's trick and dust them with cornflour not icing sugar – it won't dissolve or go sticky.

Tips from the judges

- Make sure each cream puff in the collection is uniform in size, nicely rounded, puffy, and not too large. They should be smooth and golden underneath.
- If you are not certain the puffs are completely dry inside, wait until they have finished cooking and make a small slit in one side to let the steam escape. Turn off the oven, wedge open the door and leave them in for a few minutes.
- The puffs will collapse when you open the oven door if the centres are still soft.

WILMINGTON
Lemon Butter

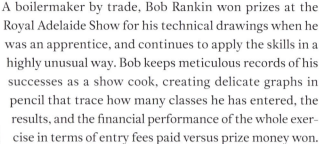

A boilermaker by trade, Bob Rankin won prizes at the Royal Adelaide Show for his technical drawings when he was an apprentice, and continues to apply the skills in a highly unusual way. Bob keeps meticulous records of his successes as a show cook, creating delicate graphs in pencil that trace how many classes he has entered, the results, and the financial performance of the whole exercise in terms of entry fees paid versus prize money won.

But it is not the money or even winning that draws Bob and his wife, Margaret, to donate so much of their energy to country shows. Besides being active competitors, they volunteer as judges, convenors and stewards, and travel to many parts of South Australia to support and promote shows. In 2006, Margaret also took on the onerous task of organising the prestigious State Rich Fruit Cake Championship and the State Genoa Cake Competition, which involves not only staging the finals at the Royal Adelaide Show, but helping eleven country shows to run regional semifinals. And Bob is promotions officer for the Agricultural Societies Council of South Australia, which represents all the shows. 'We get a lot of enjoyment out of it . . . We have met a lot of very nice people,' Bob says.

The Rankins moved to Wilmington in 1985 and joined the local show society soon after. About the same time Bob walked around the

Above: Margaret and Bob Rankin

Bottom left: One of Bob's delicate pencil graphs

Bottom right: The memorial gates into the Wilmington showground

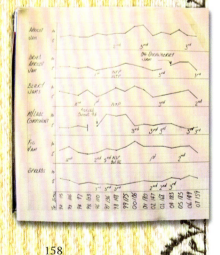

indoor section of the Royal Adelaide Show and thought he would like to have a go at making preserves, but it took perseverance to win a prize. 'We started off thinking we knew everything but we really new bugger all and it took us a long time,' he admits.

One of their favourite recipes is lemon butter, also known as lemon cheese. 'We have it down to a fairly fine art,' says Margaret who won three firsts for her lemon butter in 2007.

Now held on a Sunday so it doesn't have to compete with local sporting competitions, the Wilmington Show started in 1881. According to a report in the *Port Augusta Dispatch*, despite heavy rain in the morning some 500 people took part in the inaugural event and the 'favourable auspices under which the first show has been held may be accepted as predictive of a successful career for years to come'.

Recipe

3 eggs, well beaten
200 g sugar
juice of 1½ lemons
rind of 1 lemon, finely grated
50 g butter, melted

Combine the eggs, sugar, lemon juice and rind, and the butter, and beat thoroughly. Pour the mixture into the top of double boiler, or a bowl, and place it over a saucepan of gently boiling water; make sure the upper pan does not touch the water. Stir constantly until the mixture thickens (about 10 minutes); do not let it boil.

Spoon the lemon butter into sterilised jars while hot, and seal when it cools.

Tips from the cook

- Roll the lemon with your hand on a hard surface to loosen up the flesh and extract more juice.
- Make sure the eggs are well beaten to get a smooth butter, without flecks of egg white. The lemon rind should also be grated very finely to avoid yellow flecks.
- The length of time it takes the mixture to thicken will vary depending on the amount of pectin in the lemon juice. If the mixture fails to thicken enough, add another well-beaten egg.
- Do not allow the butter to boil or it will curdle. Never try cooking it on direct heat.
- The acidity and amount of juice in lemons vary. If your butter tastes too sweet, try adding up to ½ teaspoon of citric acid.
- If you don't measure the sugar precisely, the butter might crystalise during storage.

Tips from the judges

- Good quality lemon butter should be bright yellow in colour, with a smooth and creamy texture and a distinctive tangy lemon flavour. It must be of spreadable consistency, and not too runny.
- Consider straining the beaten eggs before adding them to the mixture to ensure they are well beaten.

WUDINNA
Honey Sponge Roll

Mavis Sampson loves working as a volunteer for organisations in her community and, at 85, believes it helps keep her active in body and mind. 'Now I am getting up in years people think I am too old but the other side of the picture is if you get involved and keep going it does you good,' Mavis says.

Recognised with a citizen of the year award in 1995 for her work with some 15 local organisations, Mavis particularly likes to support the Wudinna Show, which started in 1920, not long after the district was settled. The first event was held on several different sites, with indoor exhibits at the town's newly completed Institute Hall. The show moved to its current ground in 1951, centred around a new oval which was later recognised as one of the best playing fields in the state, hosting games between Adelaide football clubs and a test match featuring the English cricket team. Today's show continues to offer a diverse program, with a food and wine tent, camp oven cook-off, shearing competition, and a ram sale.

'I often wonder how long it will keep going but once a show goes it's a big loss out of a district,' Mavis says. 'A show brings people together . . . it's given me a lot.' Mavis lived on a farm at Kyancutta for more than 60 years before moving into Wudinna in 2005. Always a keen cook, she has competed in shows across Eyre Peninsula, learning her craft by listening to the judges while volunteering as a steward. Mavis is well known for her light and delicate honey sponge roll, a favourite at family gatherings and community occasions.

Recipe

3 eggs
$1/2$ cup sugar
$1/2$ cup cornflour
2 heaped teaspoons plain flour
1 level teaspoon cream of tartar
$1/2$ level teaspoon bicarbonate of soda

1 level teaspoon mixed spice
$1/2$ teaspoon cinnamon
1 tablespoon honey, melted
300 ml cream, whipped

Preheat the oven to moderate (180 °C in a conventional electric oven). Grease a Swiss roll pan (about 25 cm by 30 cm) and line it with greaseproof paper.

Tips from the judges

- The cake should have the qualities of a sponge. There should be no stickiness on the surface, caused by the sugar not being dissolved properly during beating.
- You cannot roll a sponge correctly if the ends are crisp because it has been cooked too long. Practice in your own oven for the best results.
- The completed roll should be plump, not just folded, and there should be no cracks. Some schedules insist that it is rolled only twice, others three times – check the schedule.

Beat the eggs for about 5 minutes with an electric mixer, set on high speed. Add the sugar and beat until thick and frothy, and the sugar is completely dissolved.

Sift together three times the cornflour, flour, cream of tartar, soda, mixed spice and cinnamon. Using a whisk and stirring very gently, add first the dry ingredients to the egg mixture and then the honey.

Gently pour the mixture into the prepared pan. Bake for 10 to 15 minutes, until golden brown, and firm to the touch.

Wet a clean tea towel and ring it out tightly to remove as much moisture as possible. Spread it out on a benchtop or table, making sure it has no creases.

Turn the sponge out on to the tea towel and carefully remove the paper. Gently roll the tea towel up with the sponge inside. Let it sit for a couple of minutes to cool slightly, and then unroll it and remove the tea towel. Roll the sponge back up.

Once the sponge is cold, gently unroll it, fill with cream and roll up again.

Tips from the cook

- Once you have beaten the eggs and sugar you must handle the mixture very gently.
- Once you have added the flour and honey it is important to beat the mixture gently but thoroughly so all the dry ingredients are incorporated evenly.
- The sponge will drop if you open the oven too soon so it may take some practice to work out the ideal cooking time. Open the oven door only a little when you think the sponge is almost cooked and not before.
- The trickiest part of the process is rolling up the sponge. Roll it as soon as it comes out of the oven, and use your fingertips. Don't attempt to roll it too tightly or the sponge will crack.
- Leave the roll as long as you can before you fill it with cream – the sponge won't be so fragile to handle.
- Think about adding mashed banana to the whipped cream if you are making it for family and friends.

Opposite page: Mavis Sampson (MS)

Left: Mavis volunteering at a fundraising cake stall in Wudinna, 1999 (MS)

Above: A show book advertisement for Gifforn fuel stoves

YALLUNDA FLAT
Jubilee Cake

Above: Dot Brougham

Tips from the judges

- In a true jubilee cake, crumbing methods are always used to incorporate the butter and create the right texture.
- The cake should be well cooked right through, with no damp patches, and there should be no hard, shiny or overheated fruit showing. The crust should not be hard and over-crisp.

It took determination, and the encouragement of her late husband Wilf, to turn Dot Brougham into one of Eyre Peninsula's most respected show cooks. Dot was in her forties before she decided to enter the Lipson Show, where there was more than a little competition from a community of women renown for their cooking skills. 'It was six or seven years before I started winning consistently,' she admits, describing her first attempts as 'terrible'.

Born at Kimba, Dot grew up one of eight children on a farm at Butler. She helped to milk cows and look after her brothers before marrying Wilf in 1951 and moving to a farm near Lipson. 'I didn't know much about cake cooking when I got married . . . I learnt by reading recipes and trying them out,' she says. But her husband was the poultry convenor and she decided she might like to get involved in the show too and have a try at 'making a cake or two'. Things did not go well at the start:

> My cakes were always put at the back and that was alright when you looked at everyone else's and saw what they had done. Then I became a steward of the cookery and I learnt a lot of things from the ladies that were judging . . . It took me quite a while to get up to what I would call show standard . . . If I didn't have a husband behind me I would never have kept up doing it.

Dot went on to win prizes and trophies across the peninsula, and eventually the State Genoa Cake Competition and the State Rich Fruit Cake Championship. She became cooking convenor at Lipson and judged at most Eyre Peninsula shows. A resident of Tumby Bay since the late 1970s, Dot now focuses most effort on supporting the Yallunda Flat Show, due to celebrate its 100th event in 2013. An extremely popular show, held on picturesque grounds, it draws about 3000 patrons each spring and a healthy number of competitors in everything from computer work and dog jumping to sheaf tossing.

Dot is not certain of the exact origins of her recipe for jubilee cake, a traditional staple that is gradually disappearing from cookery schedules but deserves to be rediscovered. Quick and economical to make, it involves a different technique to other fruit cakes.

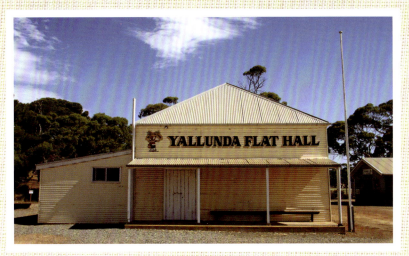

Top left: The Yallunda Flat hall

Left: The showground main gateway

Above: The 1918 Yallunda Flat show book cover; a display ad promoting the show luncheon; an advertisement encouraging entries (YFAHSI)

Top: Yallunda Flat Show, c. 1935 (SLSA: B 18483)
Above: Yallunda Flat showground, c. 1935 (SLSA: B 18484)

Recipe

65 g butter
250 g SR flour
2 dessertspoons castor sugar
pinch of salt
1/2 cup sultanas
1/2 cup currants
1 dessertspoon lemon peel

1 egg, beaten
milk

Icing
1/2 cup icing sugar
cream (enough to moisten)
water
desiccated coconut

Jubilee Cake

Preheat the oven to moderate (180 °C in a conventional electric oven).

Grease and line a 23 cm by 8 cm log pan.

Rub the butter into the flour, sugar and salt until the mixture resembles fine breadcrumbs. Add the sultanas, currants, lemon peel and stir through the flour mixture.

Beat the egg in a measuring cup and then top the cup up with milk. Add to the flour mixture and mix until combined, forming a fairly stiff mixture.

Spoon it evenly into the prepared pan and bake for 35 minutes, or until golden. Remove the cake from the pan and place it on a board to cool. While it is still warm, pour the icing over the cake so it drizzles down the sides. Finish with a light sprinkling of coconut.

Icing
Beat together the icing sugar and just enough cream to moisten it. Then add enough water to make a slightly runny consistency.

Tips from the cook

- Use a food processor to 'crumb' the flour, sugar and butter.
- Dot always adds a pinch of salt to her cakes to 'bring out the flavour'.
- Coating the fruit in the flour mixture before adding any liquid helps distribute the fruit more evenly and stops it from sinking.
- The top of the cake has to be quite rough so don't smooth it out once you have worked the mixture into the pan.
- Mixing the icing with cream stops it from lifting off the cake.

YANKALILLA
Chicken Cheesecake

Jill Chinner helped thousands of Australians become better cooks. A cookery demonstrator, television presenter, teacher, author, champion darts player and committed community volunteer, she started her career in 1954 as a trainee home economist with the Electricity Trust of South Australia (ETSA), travelling across the state to give cooking demonstrations and help people learn how to use their electric stoves.

After taking a break from paid work to raise three children, Jill taught on a part-time basis for TAFE and the South Australian Gas Company, acted as a consultant to the then Australian Meat and Livestock Corporation, and gave cookery demonstrations promoting 'new-fashioned pork'. She produced cookbooks and recipes for the South Australian Egg Board and was the voice at the end of the telephone help-line for owners of Fowlers preserving kits.

When Australian bush painter and adventurer Jack Absolam decided to create a barbecue cookbook, Jill was co-author. 'She spent a week in the bush out of Broken Hill with a film crew and Jack, and actually did all the cooking in the barbecues and camp ovens for photography,' recalls husband Tony. She was also a regular presenter on Channel 10's *Touch of Elegance*, and catered for everything from major conferences to church camps before setting up Fleurieu Fine Foods at Yankalilla in 1991. The highly successful business produced gourmet jams and preserves which were exported overseas and dished up on flights by Qantas and Cathay Pacific.

Jill was a regular judge at the Royal Adelaide Show and country shows as far as Alice Springs, and a much-valued member of the Yankalilla Rapid Bay and Myponga Agricultural and Horticultural Society, serving as secretary, cookery convenor and coordinator of the show kiosk until her unexpected death in May 2007 at the age of 67. Her family agreed to provide one of her favourite recipes in tribute, after discovering it in the collection of thousands she left behind. 'Everyone who tasted it wanted the recipe but she kept it a secret,' Tony says.

Jill was the latest in a long line of women who have contributed to the Yankalilla Show Society since it was founded in 1882. The society's first event was noted for its special prizes for cats, locally made boots and shoes, shearing, and the best Merino ram. A few years later permanent grounds were bought and a hall built, providing an important ongoing venue for the local community.

Recipe

Base
125 g plain unsalted biscuits, crumbed
90 g butter, melted
2 teaspoons mixed herbs

Filling
250 g cream cheese, softened
3 eggs, separated
1/3 cup cream
30 g butter
1 onion, finely chopped
2 tablespoons plain flour
2/3 cup chicken stock
90 g matured cheese, grated
1 teaspoon dry mustard
salt and black pepper
1/2 cup chopped ham
2 cups chopped, cooked chicken

Mushroom Sauce
3 teaspoons butter
6 mushrooms, sliced
2 tablespoons cream
60 g matured cheese, grated
parsley, chopped

Preheat oven to moderate (180 °C in a conventional electric oven).

To make the base, mix the biscuit crumbs with the butter and herbs. Press over the base of a greased 25 cm springform pan.

To make the filling, beat the cream cheese in a small bowl until smooth; then beat in the egg yolks and cream. Place the butter and onion in a pan and sauté until soft. Stir in the flour and then gradually blend in the stock. Simmer until thickened, stirring continuously. Add the cheese, mustard, and salt and pepper to taste. Stir in the cream cheese mixture, the ham and the chicken until combined. Beat the egg whites until stiff peaks form. Fold the egg whites gently into the chicken filling.

Pour the filling over the prepared base and cook for 1–1 1/2 hours, or until golden and firm.

Mushroom Sauce
Place the butter and mushrooms in a pan and sauté until softened; add the cream and cheese, stirring until the cheese melts.

Remove the cheesecake from the pan and place on a serving platter. Top with the mushroom sauce and sprinkle with parsley.
SERVES 8 TO 10 PEOPLE.

Tips from the cook's family

- Serve the cheesecake with a simple tossed salad.

Opposite page, top: Jill and Tony Chinner

Opposite page, bottom: A horse competitor at the Yankalilla Show (TT)

Below: A show book advertisement for John Martin food hall

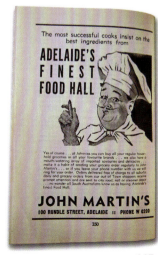

SED for
GING

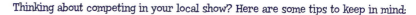

How to be a Prizewinning Show Cook

Thinking about competing in your local show? Here are some tips to keep in mind:

- Read your show book schedule very carefully – read it when you are deciding which classes to enter, read it again before you start cooking, and then read it again to make sure you meet all the specifications given for the section and class. In particular, check the requirements for pan sizes, number of items in a collection, and presentation.

- The main criteria judges generally use to assess entries include colour, texture, aroma, flavour, and overall appearance and presentation. While appearance is important it is not everything – judges cut, sniff, crumble and taste entries to decide the winners.

- Always use the highest quality ingredients.

- Get to know your oven – every oven is different, so recipes can only ever provide a guide to temperatures and cooking times as a starting point.

- Use clean, dry cake pans without wrinkles or dents. Traditionally, judges have preferred that cake pan corners are sharp, rather than rounded, although it is becoming increasingly difficult to source this type of pan and many judges are prepared to take this into account. However, if you are thinking about taking on the major cake competitions, it would be a good idea to look for this type of pan.

- Leaving the pan lining on the bottom of your cake, or any sign of wire rack marks are regarded as major faults in show cooking. One of the first things a judge will do is tip your cake upside down to check the bottom.

- Schedules usually indicate whether a show will provide plates on which to stand your cookery entries, or which type of plate to use. If no instructions are provided, use plain, white paper plates.

- Try to avoid using a thick skewer to test whether your cake is cooked – it will leave a channel. Try a small thin skewer or knitting needle, or even a piece of fuse wire.

- Judges will cut or break every cookery entry to check the texture, even distribution of ingredients, and whether it is cooked through properly.

- If the cake has to be decorated, use a moderate amount of icing and apply it neatly.

- Entries need to be even in colour, including the bottom and sides. For cakes and pastries, avoid using dark pans or adonised trays for cooking. Shiny aluminium trays or pans are best.

- Do not use a packet cake mixture, unless you are entering a class that is specifically for packet cakes.

- When showing bottled preserves, make sure the jars or bottles are clean and shiny, and check for stipulations about container size.

- Most shows allow for preserves to be sealed with either lids or cellophane.

- Spreadibility or consistency is an important feature for jams, marmalades, chutneys, relishes and sauces. Judges will also be assessing the colour and flavour.

- Consider volunteering as a steward at your local show so you can learn firsthand from more experienced cooks, and the judges.

- Don't give up – many of the cooks featured in this book speak despairingly of their early efforts, but they persevered and actively sought advice from other cooks, stewards and judges about how to improve.

- If you are not certain about what is required for your local show, contact the cookery or preserves convenors, who are usually listed in the show book.

- For extensive information, look for two books written by experienced competitors and judges: *Cooking for Competition*, by Joan Graham and Doreen Moore, which covers important aspects for cookery classes; and *The Show Bench*, by Joan Graham, which focuses on confectionary, produce and preserves.

Guide to Image Credits

*all other photographs taken by the author, Liz Harfull

AAHFSI = courtesy of the Angaston Agricultural, Horticultural and Floricultural Society Incorporated

AGASA = S.T. Gill Australia, 1818–1880 *Agricultural and Horticultural Show, Adelaide* 1843, Adelaide watercolour on paper 20.8 x 30.8 cm. Gift of M.J.M. Carter AO through the Art Gallery of South Australia Foundation 2004. Art Gallery of South Australia, Adelaide.

BH = photograph by Belinda Hansen

CAHSI = courtesy of the Cummins Agricultural and Horticultural Society Incorporated

DO = courtesy of Denise Ogilvy

EDAHSI = from *Eudunda Show Centenary: A History 1896 to 1997*, reproduced with permission of the Eudunda and District Agricultural and Horticultural Society Incorporated

GAHFSI = courtesy of the Gawler Agricultural, Horticultural and Floricultural Society Incorporated

GJ = courtesy of Grace James

HF = courtesy of the Harfull family

HW = photograph by heidi who? photos

JH = courtesy of John Hinze

KAHFSI = courtesy of the Kadina Agricultural, Horticultural and Floricultural Society Incorporated

KAPHSI = courtesy of the Kingston Agricultural, Pastoral and Horticultural Society Incorporated

KC = photograph by Kerri Cliff, Fresh Eyre Photography

KH = courtesy of Kathleen Herrmann

KTDSSI = courtesy of the Keith and Tintinara District Show Society Incorporated

LAHSI = courtesy of the Loxton Agricultural and Horticultural Society Incorporated

MAHFSI = courtesy of the Maitland Agricultural, Horticultural and Floricultural Society Incorporated

MBAHSI = courtesy of the Murray Bridge Agricultural and Horticultural Society Incorporated

MBASI = courtesy of the Mount Barker Agricultural Society Incorporated

MD = courtesy of Margaret Douglas

MK = courtesy of Mavis Klitscher

MNTM = courtesy of the Minlaton National Trust Museum

MPAHFSI = courtesy of the Mount Pleasant Agricultural, Horticultural and Floricultural Society Incorporated

MRAS = courtesy of the Mount Remarkable Agricultural Society (Melrose)

MS = courtesy of Mavis Sampson

N/AA = ©Newspix/Adelaide *Advertiser* newspaper

NA = courtesy of the *Northern Argus* newspaper, Clare

NTSA = courtesy of the National Trust of South Australia

OF = courtesy of the Ogilvie family

OHS = courtesy of the Orroroo Historical Society

PC = courtesy of Prue Clark

PR = photograph by Pauline Rivetts

RAHAFSA = courtesy of the Royal Agricultural and Horticultural Archives Foundation of South Australia

RH = photograph by Roger Harfull

SM = courtesy of Sue McCallum

SRM = courtesy of the Swan Reach Museum

SYPASI = courtesy of the Southern Yorke Peninsula Agricultural Society Incorporated

TBC = courtesy of *The Border Chronicle* newspaper

TBW = courtesy of *The Border Watch* newspaper, Mount Gambier

TF = photograph by Tim Froling

TFr = photograph by Terry Faulkner

TI = courtesy of the *The Islander* newspaper, Kangaroo Island

TT = courtesy of *The Times* newspaper, Victor Harbor

USHFSI = from *Reminiscences of 100 Uraidla Shows*, published by Uraidla and Summertown Horticultural and Floricultural Society Incorporated

VS = photograph by Veronica Sporn

WSSI = courtesy of the Whyalla Show Society Incorporated

YFAHSI = courtesy of the Yallunda Flat Agricultural and Horticultural Society Incorporated

YJ = photograph by Yvonne Johns

Index

Anzac Biscuits 124
Apple Squares 152
Banana Cake 58
Biscuits
    Anzac 124
    Chocolate Orange Swirls 20
    Cornflake 62
    Honey 50
    Macadamia and Wattle Seed 118
Boiled Fruit Cake 88
Bread 44
Cakes
    Banana 58
    Boiled Fruit 88
    Carrot 144
    Chocolate Cupcakes 70
    Chocolate Fudge 132
    Chocolate Layer 128
    Cinnamon Coffee 78
    Genoa 122
    German Yeast 148
    Ginger Fluff 106
    Jubilee 162
    Mango Diabetic Fruit 30
    Orange 140
    Ribbon 131
    Rich Fruit 12
    Sultana 114
Carrot Cake 144
Chicken Cheesecake 166
Chocolate Orange Swirls 20
Chocolate Crackles 38
Chocolate Cupcakes 70
Chocolate Layer Cake 128
Chocolate Peppermint Slice 92
Cinnamon Coffee Cake 78
Cockles 22
Coffee Kisses 46
Cornflake Biscuits 62
Cream Puffs 156
Cumquat Marmalade 98
Curried Zucchini Relish 36
Desserts
    Economical Steamed Plum Pudding 72
    Mumma's Rote Grütze 26
Dried Apricot Jam 116
Economical Steamed Plum Pudding 72
Eggplant and Chilli Chutney 32
Fig Jam 82
Fruit and Nut Loaf 136
Fruit Cakes
    Boiled 88
    Fruit and Nut Loaf 136
    Genoa 122
    Jubilee 162
    Mango Diabetic 30
    Rich Fruit 12
    Sultana 114
Genoa Cake 122
German Yeast Cake 148
Ginger Apricot Crunch 84
Ginger Fluff 106

Grandma's Chocolate Fudge Cake 132
Grape Jam 146
Homemade Bread 44
Honey Biscuits 50
Honey Sponge Roll 160
Jenny's Grape Jam 146
Jubilee Cake 162
Lemon Butter 158
Lemon Slice 34
Lemonade Scones 68
Macadamia and Wattle Seed Biscuits 118
Mango Diabetic Fruit Cake 30
Mary's Farm Pasties 110
Maud's Ginger Apricot Crunch 84
Moderator's Slice 138
Mustard Pickle
Mumma's Rote Grütze 26
Nestor's Yeast Buns 94
Orange Cake 140
Pasties 110
Pastry
    Cream Puffs 156
    Pasties 110
    Sausage Rolls 102
Pinch of Salt Sponge 86
Plum Pudding 72
Preserves
    Cumquat Marmalade 98
    Curried Zucchini Relish 36
    Dried Apricot Jam 116
    Eggplant and Chilli Chutney 32
    Fig Jam 82
    Grape Jam 146
    Lemon Butter 158
    Mustard Pickle 66
    Quince Jelly 48

Tomato Sauce 24
Quince Jelly 48
Raspberry Jam Roll 74
Rich Fruit Cake 12
Ribbon Cake 131
Rock Buns 54
Rote Grütze 26
Sausage Rolls 102
Savouries
    Chicken Cheesecake 166
    Pasties 110
    Sausage Rolls 102
    Savoury Scones 69
Scones
    Lemonade 68
    Savoury 69
Slices
    Apple Squares 152
    Chocolate Peppermint 92
    Ginger Apricot Crunch 84
    Lemon 34
    Moderator's 138
Sponges
    Ginger Fluff 106
    Honey Roll 160
    Pinch of Salt 86
    Raspberry Jam Roll 74
Sue's Sausage Rolls 102
Sultana Cake 114
Tomato Sauce 24
Zucchini, Apple and Carrot Muffins 42
Yeast Buns 94
Yeast Cookery
    Bread 44
    Buns 94
    German Cake 148

Wakefield Press is an independent publisher and distribution company based in Adelaide, South Australia. We love good stories and publish beautiful books. To see our full range of titles, please visit our website at www.wakefieldpress.com.au.